Walk There!

50 Treks in and around Portland and Vancouver

Edited by Laura O. Foster • Illustrations by Eben Dickinson

About Metro
People places. Open spaces.

As your elected regional government, Metro is helping to make the region an extraordinary place to live, work and play. *Walk There!* is a project of Metro's Regional Travel Options program. The program carries out regional strategies to increase use of travel options, reduce pollution and improve mobility. Regional travel options include all of the alternatives to driving alone – carpooling, vanpooling, riding transit, bicycling, walking and telecommuting. Visit www.oregonmetro.gov to learn more.

Metro Representatives

Metro Council President:	David Bragdon
Metro Councilors:	Rex Burkholder, Carl Hosticka, Robert Liberty, Kathryn Harrington, Carlotta Collette, Rod Park
Auditor:	Suzanne Flynn

Safety Responsibility

Walking routes depicted are advisory and illustrative. Metro has not undertaken any independent safety review of the sidewalks, trails and facilities. Users of this guidebook expressly agree that their use is at their sole risk. Guide users also assume the entire risk as to the quality and accuracy of the guide. Metro disclaims any responsibility for errors, omissions or inaccuracies in this guide. In no event shall Metro be held liable for any damages or loss of any kind related to the information in this guidebook.

Metro
600 NE Grand Avenue, Portland, OR 97232
503-797-1700
ISBN-13: 978-0-9662473-9-8

Printed in the United States of America.

Mixed Sources
Product group from well-managed forests, controlled sources and recycled wood or fiber
www.fsc.org Cert no. SCS-COC-001142
© 1996 Forest Stewardship Council

This book is funded in part by Kaiser Permanente and the Federal Transit Administration.

Contents

(continued on page 4)

East Region (continued from page 3)

Gresham

Troutdale

Clackamas County

Milwaukie

Portland

South Region

Lake Oswego

Oregon City

West Linn

Wilsonville

South Region (continued from page 4)

Foreword

Even in our modern industrial age, we continue to discover that one of the most important means of transportation is... the human foot. Walking is great for our health, easy on the environment and free of charge. Traveling by foot connects us to each other and the place we call home. Neighborhoods and metropolitan regions are at their best when people can and do walk.

All the residents of the Portland-Vancouver metropolitan area should have access to sidewalks and trails that take us from the places we live to the places we learn, work, shop and play. Each of us should be able to trace a path from our front door to one of the magnificent rivers, creeks, buttes, forests and natural areas that distinguish our region.

There's work to be done to turn this bold vision – shared and shaped by generations of Oregonians and Washingtonians – into reality. Key gaps must be filled to finally complete an interconnected network of trails more than 100 years in the making. Governments need to plan and maintain sidewalks, paths and trails and invest transportation tax dollars in expanding travel options.

Working together – governments, nonprofits and volunteers, and organizations like Kaiser Permanente – we can achieve more. That's one reason the Metro Council has joined with other public and private organizations in a Connecting Green Alliance. Visit www.oregonmetro.gov/connectinggreen for more information.

We have a collective responsibility to improve our trails and walkways. In return, we get to enjoy the personal reward of using them. So let this guide introduce you to some of our region's fascinating places and tremendous natural beauty.

David Bragdon, *President, Metro Regional Council*

Introduction

Did you know that one of the easiest, most effective activities you can do to tighten your wallet and your waistline is right at the tips of your toes?

Walking is good for your wallet. If you drive less, you save more by avoiding the costs of gasoline, parking and wear and tear on your vehicle. It's an economical way to shop, run errands or visit friends. According to the National Household Travel Survey, 25 percent of trips in the United States are 0.25 mile or less. Try walking the next time you're heading for your local coffee shop—you may be pleasantly surprised that it's not as far away as you thought.

Walking is one of the safest activities you can do to maintain your health. Increasing your physical activity increases your energy level and can help you lose or maintain weight. Mile for mile, you can burn as many calories walking as you would jogging, but with far less stress on your joints. Walking is also a weight-bearing exercise, which means it strengthens the bones and muscles in your lower body.

Walking is also good for your emotional health, giving you a break from the stress of driving. You can get out in nature and neighborhoods and have time to really look at your surroundings. Invite family members or friends to walk with you, and you get to spend more quality time with them and strengthen your relationships.

Plus, walking helps the environment. Reduce your carbon footprint by shifting short trips from your car to your own feet or by using mass transit. Walking a few minutes to a bus stop takes the same amount of time as warming up the car or searching for a parking spot.

So put on a pair of good shoes and head out the door! Whether you're strolling around your neighborhood or exploring a new area, you'll have fun, and your wallet, body and world will thank you for it.

KAISER PERMANENTE® thrive

TAKE THE ROAD
LESS TRAVELED.

How to Use this Book

Walk There! is laid out in four color-coded regional sections. Each regional section begins with a map of walks within that area and a summary list that conveniently categorizes the walks as:

Nature in Neighborhoods Walk
Explore parks, trails and scenic places close to home.

Power Walk
Challenge yourself with longer distances and elevated terrain.

City Cruise
Explore city centers and commercial districts.

History Walk
Learn about the region's rich history.

Lunchtime Stroll
Walk over level terrain in short one-hour routes, suitable for people with mobility assistance devices or strollers.

Many routes offer a variety of experiences and are listed under more than one category. Please note that the walks have not been checked for compliance with ADA accessibility guidelines.

An information bar on the first page of each route lists the **GPS coordinates** in decimal degrees for the start location as well as the walk's **length in miles**, **difficulty rating** and **number of steps.** Most routes are loops, and mileage for the total loop is given. When routes are out-and-back excursions, round-trip mileage is given. The difficulty rating takes into account both distance and elevation gain. The number of steps is based upon an average stride of 2.5 feet for 2,112 steps per mile; your actual number of steps may vary based on the length of your stride.

Every *Walk There!* route begins and ends near a bus or MAX light rail stop. Transit information is provided on page 10. For more information on walking resources, visit **www.oregonmetro.gov/walk** and see page 232.

Legend

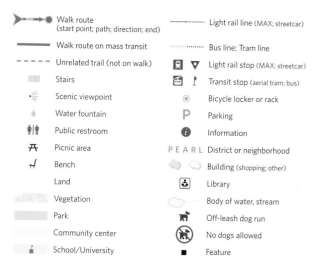

- Walk route (start point; path; direction; end)
- Walk route on mass transit
- Unrelated trail (not on walk)
- Stairs
- Scenic viewpoint
- Water fountain
- Public restroom
- Picnic area
- Bench
- Land
- Vegetation
- Park
- Community center
- School/University

- Light rail line (MAX; streetcar)
- Bus line; Tram line
- Light rail stop (MAX; streetcar)
- Transit stop (aerial tram; bus)
- Bicycle locker or rack
- P Parking
- *i* Information
- PEARL District or neighborhood
- Building (shopping; other)
- Library
- Body of water, stream
- Off-leash dog run
- No dogs allowed
- ■ Feature

Getting There

Every *Walk There!* route begins and ends near a bus or MAX light rail stop. Use TriMet's Trip Planner to plan your trip and TransitTracker™ to find out exactly when your ride is coming. Access both at www.trimet.org or call 503-238-RIDE (7433). SMART (South Metro Area Regional Transit) operates routes that serve Wilsonville and make connections to TriMet; visit www.ridesmart.com or call 503-682-7790. For Vancouver and Clark County, Washington walks, visit C-TRAN at www.c-tran.com or call 360-695-0123. Please note that bus routes and schedules change annually. Check with your transit provider before you head out.

Consider using transit to incorporate walking into your daily activities. Try exiting the bus one stop early to get in extra steps.

North Region

	D	N	P	C	H	L
A. Vancouver: Burnt Bridge Creek Greenway p. 13	4.0	•				
B. Vancouver: Fort, Downtown and Waterfront p. 17	3.96			•	•	
C. Vancouver: Salmon Creek Greenway p. 21	6.2	•	•		•	
D. Portland: Alameda Ridge and Stairs p. 25	4.4		•	•	•	
E. Portland: Hollywood Center p. 29	0.9			•		•
F. Portland: Irvington p. 33	2.8			•	•	•
G. Portland: Kenton to Columbia Slough p. 37	4.6	•		•	•	
H. Portland: King Neighborhood p. 41	1.9			•	•	
I. Portland: Laurelhurst p. 45	3.5			•	•	•
J. Portland: Lloyd District and Sullivan's Gulch p. 49	1.0			•	•	
K. Portland: Mississippi and Overlook p. 53	2.1	•		•	•	•
L. Portland: Pearl District and Nob Hill p. 57	3.3			•	•	
M. Portland: Pearl District to Pittock Mansion p. 61	5.6		•	•	•	
N. Portland: Peninsula Park and 4 ... p. 65	2.6	•		•	•	•
O. Portland: Swan Island Beach p. 69	4.4	•			•	•

D Distance in Miles   C City Cruise
N Nature Walk   H History Walk
P Power Walk   L Lunchtime Stroll

Vancouver
Burnt Bridge Creek Greenway

This walk showcases the westernmost 2 miles (one-way) of the 8-mile Burnt Bridge Creek Trail, a paved, multiuse trail that follows the path of Burnt Bridge Creek through the northern stretches of Vancouver. The trail passes through forests and grassland and accesses two city parks.

Begin at Stewart Glen, located at the mouth of Burnt Bridge Creek, at Fruit Valley Road and Bernie Drive. The creek here, before it enters Vancouver Lake, is impounded by road and railroad embankments, making for good bird habitat in winter. The trail meanders east along the creek through thick forest and bottomlands. To visit Kiggins Bowl, at Hazel Dell Avenue turn right and walk south. Kiggins Bowl, named for a former Vancouver mayor, features a track, football field and tree-lined walkways.

To continue east on the trail, watch for a trail connection on the east side of Hazel Dell Avenue. This trail allows you to cross I-5 on a pedestrian/bicycle overpass. At the east end of the overpass, head south to Leverich Park. Here you'll find open fields, forest, picnic areas and a quaint footbridge over the creek. The trail continues east another 6 miles.

See www.cityofvancouver.us/parks-recreation/parks_trails for information about other access points.

4.0 miles : 8448 steps : ▮▮▮▮ difficulty : ◈ 45.673, -122.691

NW 25t
NW 69th St
Ave

Stewart Glen
trailhead

Lakeview

NW Overlook Dr

NW Anderson Ave

NW Fruit Valley Rd

NW Dogwood Dr

NW Bernie Dr

Heather
Gate
Ridge

Burnt
Bridge
Creek
Greenway

Vancouver
Lake
Park

NW 62nd St

NW 62nd
St

NW Cherry St

NW Garfield Ave

NW Lincoln Ave

NW 59th St

NW 58th St

Franklin
Park

NW Walnut St

NW 53rd St

NW 53rd St

NW Franklin St

Benjamin
Franklin

Dugan

NW 44th

VANCOUVER: BURNT BRIDGE CREEK GREENWAY

N

| 0 | ¼ | ½ miles |
| 0 | 1320 | 2640 feet |

NW 4

Stewart Glen

Burnt Bridge Creek once served as Vancouver's water supply, until city wells were dug. Donald and Betty Stewart donated 12 acres of land on the creek to be preserved as a natural arboretum and wildlife refuge. The Stewarts's donation was a catalyst in the formation of what became the "Stewart Glen" area of Burnt Bridge Creek. It is home to deer, coyote, rabbit, raccoon and feral cats.

Leverich Park's northern parking lot offers access to the multiuse Ellen Davis Trail. It passes through the propagation gardens of the J. D. Ross Complex; plants started here were transplanted to the grounds of Bonneville Dam and other power generating sites and stations. Orchard trees and other landscape plants, from a farm that predated the Ross Complex, create good bird habitat. This trail continues up a steep grade on the way to Vancouver's Minnehaha neighborhood before ending at St. James Road.

Burnt Bridge Creek

Vancouver
Fort, Downtown and Waterfront

This walk is rich in history, passing through the Vancouver National Historic Reserve (VNHR) and downtown Vancouver, then traveling over a unique 40-foot long land bridge.

Begin at the VNHR Visitor Center, 1501 E. Evergreen Boulevard. Walk west on Evergreen along Officers' Row, home to the U.S. Army's Vancouver Barrack's officer corps from the 1850s until the post's reduction in size and scope after World War II. Cross I-5 and enter downtown Vancouver.

From Evergreen, turn left onto Esther Street and pass through a vibrant urban renewal area, home of the Vancouver Farmers Market. From Esther, walk into Esther Short Park. Leave the park at the glockenspiel in its southeast corner and walk south on Columbia Street. It bends left and passes under the Interstate Bridge. Follow the pathway along the Columbia River, passing interpretive panels highlighting Fort Vancouver's days as a fur trading headquarters, the Oregon Trail and the arrival of the U.S. Army.

Leave the river at Old Apple Tree Park, and proceed to the pedestrian land bridge spanning State Route 14. Follow the bridge to the fort site and uphill to the Visitor Center. For a longer walk, continue east along the river, then turn north on Columbia Shores Boulevard. Walk under SR 14 to connect with V Street. Turn left on 5th, right on E Reserve Street, and then left on Evergreen to return to the start.

3.96 miles : **8730** steps : ▮▮▮▮ difficulty : ◈ 45.628, -122.663

E 12th St
E 11th St

E Mill Plain Blvd

E Reserve St

Officers' Row

E 9th St

Grace St

U St

W St

E 9th St

X St

Evergreen Arboretum

T St

E 8th St

E 8th St

Vancouver National Historic Reserve Visitor Center

E Evergreen   Blvd

R St   S St

E 6th St

X St

E 6th St

E Reserve St

Davis Ave

E 5th St

V St

Pearson Air Museum

E 4th St   R St

E 3rd Lp

V St   X St

E 2nd St

Pearson Field

E 1st St   Y St

V St

s And Clark Highway

SE Columbia Way

Columbia House Blvd

(14)

SE Cutter Ln

Columbia River Trail

SE Maritime Ave

SE Columbia River Dr

SE Hidden Way

The Confluence Project

The land bridge is part of the Confluence Project, seven art installations in the Columbia River Basin that evoke the history of the Lewis and Clark Expedition of 1804–1806 and the changes it brought to the peoples and landscape of the Pacific Northwest.

At the bridge are two cedar canoe panels that reference the site's role as a historic tribal crossroads as well as a point of contact between European and Native people. The bridge was designed by Seattle architect Johnpaul Jones, and is near the terminus of the "Klickitat Trail" that linked interior Klickitat and Taidnapam people to the riverine Chinook people, and linked river resources (smelt, sturgeon, salmon, wapato) with those of the prairies and mountains (camas, oak, berries, game animals). The bridge also reconnects Fort Vancouver's fort site and gardens with sites along the river where much of the working life of the fort took place from the 1820s to the 1840s.

Aerial view of the land bridge

Vancouver: Salmon Creek Greenway

This 3.1-mile one-way paved trail in West Vancouver winds along the banks of Salmon Creek. The 850 acres of the greenway, opened to the public in 1996, include forest, creeks, meadows and ponds. Along the path are wildlife interpretive areas, duck nesting boxes and restored habitat. If you like birding, bring binoculars.

Access the greenway from either end. The east end access is at Salmon Creek Park, 1112 NE 117th Street. The west end access is at the Felida Bridge, at NW 36th Avenue's crossing of Salmon Creek. Transit access is easiest at the west end.

Beginning at the east end, at Salmon Creek Park, is Klineline Pond. Once a gravel pit, it is now a spring-fed lake with a sandy beach and lifeguards in summer. The park has 35 developed acres and 368 acres of undeveloped natural area.

The Salmon Creek Greenway trail leads west from the park. The creek itself consists of two habitat subtypes: a free-flowing stream that responds to rainfall cycles, with main channels and meandering overflow channels, and the tidal Columbia River backwater. Small ponds contain waterfowl throughout the year. Benches along the trail invite you to sit quietly and watch the rich wildlife scene.

An optional out and back walk is the .5 mile long Cougar Creek Trail on the south side of the Salmon Creek Greenway at about the midway point. Cougar Creek is the first major tributary upstream from the mouth of Salmon Creek. Riparian woodlands remain along much of the deep ravine in its lower reaches.

6.2 miles : **13094** steps : ▮▮▮▮ difficulty : ◀◈▶ 45.707, -122.668

NW Bliss Rd

NW 26th Ave

NW 143rd St

NW 21st Ave

NW 31st Ct

NW 29th Ave

NW 27th Ave NW

Bosch

NW Seward Rd

NW 23rd Ct

Pinecrest

NW 138th St

NW Hathaway Rd

NW 36th Ave

NW 16th Ave

NW 11th Ave

NW 136th St

Salmon Creek Greenway

NW 134th St

NW 133rd St

82nd Cir

NW 131st Way

NW 30th Ct

NW 35th Ct

NW 28th Ave

NW 131st

NW 25th Ct

NW129th Cir

NW 25th Ave

NW 128th St

NW 21st Ave

NW 127th St

NW 127th St

NW 20th Ave

NW 19th Ave

NW 124th St

NW 31st Ave

NW 15th Ave

NW 124th St

NW 124th St

NW 11th Ct NW 11th Ave

NW 124th St

Cougar Creek Trail

NW 21st Ave

NW 120th St

NW 119th St

NW 16th Ave

Burton Forest

NW Lakeshore Ave

Cougar Creek Greenway

VANCOUVER: SALMON CREEK GREENWAY

N

0   ¼   ½ miles

0   1320   2640 feet

A Name Game

Salmon Creek runs through Felida, now part of Vancouver, but once a farming and orchard community. In 1890, a name was needed for the small community northeast of Vancouver Lake. Local lore says that the name "Powley" was submitted to postal authorities; the name was denied and authorities gave an alternate: "Polly." The postmaster of the area, C. C. Lewis, responded in disgust, saying the name sounded like a parrot; if that's what was wanted, he said, why not use the name of his cat. So he submitted "Thomas," his cat's name, as well as Tomcat and Felidae, the Latin name for cat. Felida it was.

The Salmon Creek Greenway is one of the largest watersheds in Clark County; its waters flow into Lake River, the Vancouver Lake Lowlands and ultimately the Columbia River. On Salmon Creek, a dam located where I-5 now crosses blocked annual salmon runs. Locals would fish there with pitchforks, picking fish out of the water and hauling them away by the wheelbarrow load.

Salmon Creek Greenway

Portland
Alameda Ridge and Stairs

Enjoy city views and boost your heart rate climbing hidden public stairways in the lovely Alameda neighborhood. This 4.4-mile loop includes a turnaround block at a 1927 mansion built by lumber baron Thomas Autzen. The walk's many stairs, beautiful homes and great views make it a fun alternative to the stair machine at the gym.

Begin at the post office at NE 50th Avenue and Sandy Boulevard. Turn left on 50th; at the dead-end, climb 43 stairs to Wistaria Drive. Turn right at the top and walk up to the intersection of Alameda and Wistaria. Turn left onto Alameda and then left to walk downhill on Wiberg Lane.

From Wiberg, turn right on Wistaria and walk west to 42nd. Cross to the south side of the street and continue on Wistaria. Cross 39th and continue on Wistaria to 38th, to a set of 78 stairs across from the house at 3041. They take you back up the ridge. At the top, turn left on Alameda; at 38th, turn left onto Klickitat and descend again from the ridge. Cross 33rd at the crosswalk and continue to 30th. Turn right; cross Fremont and climb 95 steps at 3011 Fremont. At the top, turn left onto Alameda Terrace. At Hamblet and 29th, stay west on Alameda Street to the triangular block bounded by Alameda, Hamblet, 26th and 24th.

(continued on page 28)

4.4 miles : **9293** steps : ▮▮▮▮▮ difficulty : ◈ 45.539, -122.611

Wilshire Park

NE Shaver St

ALAMEDA

NE Alameda St

NE Fremont St

NE Klickitat St

NE Merges

NE Siskiyou St

NE Siskiyou St

NE Morris St

NE Brazee Ct

NE Brazee St

NE Knott St

GRANT PARK

NE Hollyro

NE Sta

Grant Park Pool

Grant Park

Grant HS

PORTLAND: ALAMEDA RIDGE AND STAIRS

N

0	1/8	1/4 miles
0	660	1320 feet

Return to 26th and Alameda and cross Alameda to Stuart Drive. To the east of 2532 Alameda is a staircase. Descend its 75 steps and turn left on Ridgewood Drive. At 26th, fork left and walk uphill (again!) on Regents Drive. Turn right at Edgehill Place and left on Fremont. Walk east eight blocks and turn right at Alameda. At 41st, cross to the north sidewalk of Alameda, then cross to Siskiyou. Turn right on 42nd to Alameda and then left to continue on Alameda. Between 4438 and 4420 is a 115-step staircase that descends to Wistaria. At the bottom, turn left and walk east. Take another staircase of 30 steps that connects lower Wistaria and 49th Avenue. At the bottom of the steps, turn left and walk to the 43 steps back down to 50th and the starting point.

Staircase off Alameda

Portland
Hollywood Center

This walk through the Hollywood neighborhood is short, but offers enough places to stop, shop and eat that it can take all day. Centered on Sandy Boulevard, the route explores buildings from this popular, close-in neighborhood's early days to its newest additions.

Begin at the Hollywood Transit Center, NE Halsey and 42nd Avenue. Cross Halsey and turn left. Walk one block and turn right on 41st. Cross Broadway and walk through the parking lot for the Hollywood Theater. Built in 1926, the theater gave its name to the neighborhood. Cross Sandy Boulevard at 41st and then turn left on Sandy. (Before you turn left, don't miss the wildly ornamented façade of the theater.) Walk one block on Sandy and turn right on 40th. Walk two blocks and turn right on Tillamook. At 41st and Tillamook is the Hollywood branch of the Multnomah County Library; people who like books can live above it.

From Tillamook, turn right on 42nd and pass several antique stores that offer a great place to spend an hour. At 42nd and Hancock, on the left is Harold Kelly Plaza. At 42nd and Sandy is the tiny Hollywood Burger Bar building. It was constructed in the 1920s as a stop for the trolley that ran on Sandy Boulevard. Cross Sandy at 42nd, turn right on 43rd , then right at Broadway and left at 42nd to return to the Transit Center.

0.9 miles | **1900** steps | difficulty | 45.534, -122.621

84

NE 40th Ave

NE Sandy Blvd Frontage Rd

Sandy Blvd

NE 41st Ave

Hollywood /
NE 42nd Ave TC
MAX Station

NE 42nd Ave

NE

Hollywood TC Access

NE Halsey St

NE Weidler St

NE Broadway

N

PORTLAND: HOLLYWOOD CENTER

0   0
         330
1/16
660 feet
1/8 miles

NE 44th Ave

NE 40th Ave

Hollywood
Senior
Center

Hollywood
Library

NE Tillamook St

NE 41st Ave

NE 42nd Ave

NE 43rd Ave

NE Sandy Blvd

NE

NE 44th Ave

Hollywood
Farmers
Market

Hancock St

Sandy Boulevard

The first use of "Sandy" as an Oregon place name was by Lewis and Clark in 1805, when they named the Quicksand River for the large deposits of sand it carried to its confluence with the Columbia. By 1850, the name had been shortened to "Sandy River." A road from the then separate town site of East Portland toward the mouth of the Sandy River was later called the Sandy Road.

At 42nd and Halsey, a 24-Hour Fitness was built in 2005 at the former site of Copeland Lumber. The new construction is part of a plan for the Hollywood Town Center area to increase densities along the MAX line; plans include development of Sandy Boulevard's older buildings, with offices and retail below and housing above.

● ● ●

Hollywood Theater sign

Portland
Irvington

This 2.8-mile loop tours one of Portland's most beautiful neighborhoods. More than 75 homes have been designated as historically significant, ranging from Mediterranean mansions to English cottages to Prairie Craftsman. Blocks of shopping and eating places on NE Broadway offer a great way to end this walk.

From NE 15th Avenue and Broadway, walk north on 15th. At Schuyler is the exuberantly styled 1906 Gustav Freiwald House, now a bed and breakfast. The varied roofline, polygonal bays and turret are elements of the Queen Anne style.

Continue on 15th and turn right at Thompson. Pass one of the first Prairie style homes in town, dating from 1909, at 1617 NE Thompson. The banks of casement windows are typical of the style. Turn left on 17th; at 2424 NE 17th, pass a 1922 Prairie home with its characteristic massive piers.

From 17th, turn left on Brazee and right on 16th. Walk one block to Knott and turn right on it and then left on 17th. Walk one block to Stanton, turn right and walk east seven blocks to 24th. Turn right on 24th, cross Knott and turn left on Brazee. Walk four blocks and turn right on 28th. At 2208 NE 28th is a 1925 English cottage with a stunning spider web window. Note the catslide roof over the main entrance and the rounded eaves, meant to emulate the thatched roofs of rural England. Here you are in the Grant Park neighborhood.

(continued on page 36)

2.8 miles : **5914** steps : ▮▮▮▮▮ difficulty : ◈ 45.535, -122.650

PORTLAND: IRVINGTON

N

| 0 | ⅛ | ¼ miles |
| 0 | 660 | 1320 feet |

NE 27th Ave
NE 28th Ave
NE 29th Ave
NE 32nd Ave

NE 24th Ave

NE Knott St

NE 32nd Pl

NE 25th Ave
NE 26th Ave
NE Brazee Ct
NE 30th Ave
NE 31st Ave
NE 32nd Ct

NE Brazee St

NE Brazee St

NE Thompson St

G R A N T

P A R K

NE 25th Ave
NE 28th Ave
NE 32nd Ave

NE 33rd Ave

NE 26th Ave
NE 27th Ave

Fernwood
MS
NE Hancock St

NE 30th Ave

NE Schuyler St

NE Broadway

NE Weidler St

Turn around here, walk north on 28th and turn left on Thompson. At 2732 NE Thompson is a Craftsman built by contractor F. E. Bowman for his own family in 1915 on three quarters of an acre. Former Portland mayor Frank Ivancie once lived here. Note the deeply recessed porch and stonework. At 26th, reenter Irvington's boundaries. From Thompson, turn left on 25th and right on Tillamook. From Tillamook, turn left on 24th and right on Hancock. At 22nd and Hancock is the 1911 Lytle mansion, a bed and breakfast. It has Mediterranean elements (the tiled roof and stucco façade) as well as Colonial Revival (the massive Classical columns and symmetric façade). Turn left on 22nd. Walk two blocks to Broadway. Turn right and enjoy the many stores and restaurants as you return to the start.

Gustav Freiwald House

Portland
Kenton to Columbia Slough

From historic Kenton, walk 0.5 mile along the Denver Avenue Viaduct to see the wildlife that thrives in Portland's backyard along the Columbia Slough. Watch for eagles, ducks, herons and cormorants in this area that originally was so rich in nature's bounty that it became one of the most heavily populated human settlements of the West.

Taking your bike on MAX and riding this loop is another option.

Begin at 8319 N Denver Avenue at the Kenton/N Denver Avenue MAX station. Across Interstate is Kenton's Paul Bunyan statue, a relic of Oregon's centennial celebration in 1959. Proceed north on Interstate, cross Argyle and then turn west to cross the MAX tracks. Take an immediate right onto the Denver Avenue Viaduct, constructed in 1929. Stay on its east side as the viaduct passes over industrial buildings and the Columbia Slough.

Turn right onto Schmeer Road and walk under the viaduct toward the Columbia Slough Trail. There is no sidewalk here but there is room to walk to the right above the curb. On the other side of the viaduct, take care while crossing one lane of traffic to follow signs west to the Columbia Slough Trail.

This paved trail runs north and then west to travel above the Columbia Slough on the south, with views of Portland International Raceway (PIR) to the north. Listen for native songbirds and frogs and bring binoculars to watch herons and other aquatic birds.

(continued on page 40)

4.6 miles ⋮ **9715** steps ⋮ ▮▮▮▮ difficulty ⋮ ◈ 45.584, -122.686

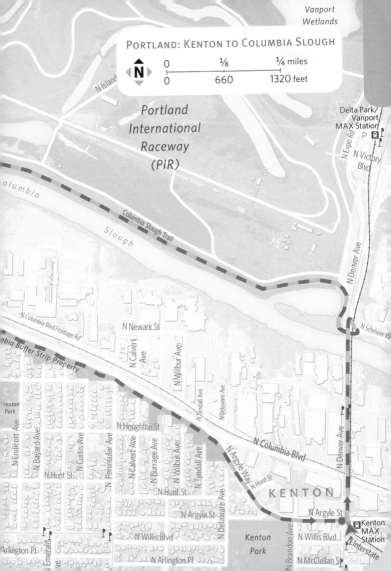

PORTLAND: KENTON TO COLUMBIA SLOUGH

N
0   ⅛   ¼ miles
0   660   1320 feet

Vanport
Wetlands

Portland
International
Raceway
(PIR)

Delta Park/
Vanport
MAX Station

N Island Ave

N Expo Rd

N Victory
Blvd

Columbia

Slough

Columbia Slough Trail

N Denver Ave

N Schmeer Rd

N Columbia Blvd Frontage Rd

N Newark St

N Calvert Ave

N Wilbur Ave

N Tyndall Ave

N Delaware Ave

bia Buffer Strip Property

Trenton
Park

N Endicott Ave

N Bayard Ave

N Curtis Ave

N Peninsular Ave

N Calvert Ave

N Burrage Ave

N Wilbur Ave

N Tyndall Ave

N Houghton St

N Hunt St

N Argyle Way

N Columbia Blvd

N Hunt St

N Denver Ave

KENTON

N Argyle St

N Delaware Ave

N Brandon Ave

N Argyle St

N Willis Blvd

Kenton
MAX
Station

Interstate

Emerald

N Willis Blvd

N Arlington Pl

Kenton
Park

N McClellan St

Continue west about 1.75 miles past Heron Lakes Golf Course and walk under a railroad overpass.

To the north is the treatment lagoon for the Columbia Boulevard Wastewater Treatment Plant. Turn south here to cross back over the slough on the Peninsula Crossing Trail pedestrian bridge and follow the trail around to the left and then south again, passing the treatment plant. Notice the wildlife themed art. One installation of metal poles could represent trees or totem poles. Another is a rock formation featuring modern petroglyphs.

From the treatment plant, turn right (west) along the trail that parallels Columbia Boulevard. Cross Columbia at the light at Portsmouth. Turn left and walk along the path, then turn off Columbia at Argyle (at a sign indicating I-5 North), angling to the right and climbing a slight hill. Stay on Argyle back to Denver. Turn right, walk a block, then cross Denver for a close-up of Paul Bunyan. The MAX station is across Interstate Avenue.

● ● ●

Paul Bunyan

Portland
King Neighborhood

The King neighborhood, one of the city's most ethnically diverse, is home to the rapidly changing NE Alberta Street and its restaurants, galleries and stores. This walk takes you down some of the neighborhood's quieter residential streets, with their century-old homes and newer infill.

Begin at the southeast corner of NE Martin Luther King Jr. Boulevard and Alberta Street. In the 1930s, this neighborhood had the city's highest concentration of foreign-born residents outside downtown, many from Germany. In the 1940s, African Americans moved here, drawn to the Northwest to work in war-time shipyards; it was one of the few city neighborhoods where non-whites were allowed to settle.

From the intersection, walk east on Alberta. At 806 is the spectacularly beautiful St. Andrew's Catholic Church, founded by Irish immigrants in 1907. The sanctuary was built in 1929 in the French Gothic style.

From Alberta, turn right on 9th; walk two blocks and turn left on Wygant; walk five blocks and turn right on 14th. In one block turn left on Going. At 1455 NE Going is a Portland Heritage Tree, a horse chestnut. From Going, turn right on 16th. In one block, turn right on Prescott and then right on 14th Place. Walk one block and turn left on Going. Follow Going west to Grand Avenue; turn right on Grand and then left on Alberta to return to the start.

1.9 miles : 4013 steps : difficulty : 45.559, -122.661

NE Webster St

NE Alberta St

NE 6th Ave

NE 9th Ave

NE Humboldt St

NE Martin Luther KingJr Blvd

NE Humboldt St

NE 7th Ave

Common
Bond
Garden

NE Wygant St

King
ES Park

NE Grand Ave

NE 8th Ave

NE Going St

NE 6th Ave

NE 10th Ave

NE Prescott St

PORTLAND: KING NEIGHBORHOOD

◀N▶

0   1/16   1/8 miles

0   330   660 feet

Street Name History

The first use of the name Alberta on a Portland street was in 1891. In that late Victorian era, the English royals were a popular discussion topic. Princess Alberta was Queen Victoria's fourth daughter; she married a nobleman who was Canada's Governor-General from 1878 to 1883. In 1882 the Province of Alberta was named for her.

Wygant Street is named for Theodore Wygant. In 1850, at 19 years of age, he was the youngest of a party of eleven that crossed the plains on a difficult trek to Oregon. On September 13, 1850, he wrote, "Killed a crow this morning; made our breakfast upon him and some coffee. Killed a few doves for dinner; ate rosebuds for dessert." Wygant settled in Oregon City and was a purser and then captain of riverboats. In 1858, he married a granddaughter of Dr. John McLoughlin.

● ● ●

St. Andrew's Catholic Church

Portland
Laurelhurst

This 3.5-mile walk loops through Laurelhurst, a residential park neighborhood from the early 1900s, where beautiful homes and heritage trees grace curving streets. The walk passes wooded Laurelhurst Park en route to the Sunny-side neighborhood with its many Queen Anne homes and lively commercial scene on SE Belmont Street.

Begin at the Belmont Library, SE 39th Avenue and Taylor Street. Walk north on 39th two blocks. Cross Belmont at the light and turn right. In one block, turn left on Peacock Lane, where Tudor style homes deck themselves out every December in a traffic-stopping light show.

At Peacock's end, turn left on Stark; walk one block and turn right on 39th and then right on Oak Court, passing a heritage Zelkova tree at 4066. Turn left on 41st and walk north six blocks to Couch. Turn left and pass a heritage Carolina poplar at 3945 and a Japanese red pine at 39th and Couch.

From Couch, turn right on 39th and walk north to Glisan where Joan of Arc gleams golden in the traffic circle. Turn right on Glisan and left on 41st. At Royal Court, turn left, cross 39th and turn left onto Imperial. From it, turn right on Laddington Court and right on Glisan. Walk three blocks and turn left on Hazelfern. A heritage American ash is at 412; a heritage monkey puzzle at 419.

(continued on page 48)

3.5 miles : 7392 steps : ▌▌▌▌▌ difficulty : ◈ 45.515, -122.622

From Hazelfern, turn left on Flanders and right on Laurelhurst Place. Walk three blocks to Burnside; cross carefully at an unmarked crossing and continue to Ankeny. Turn right and pass the 1912 mansion at 3360 designed for Russell Albee, then Portland's mayor. Next door is a 1923 Mediterranean mansion.

From Ankeny, turn left on 33rd. Cross Stark and enter the Sunnyside neighborhood. From 33rd, turn left on Alder and then right on 34th. At Belmont, turn right, passing the old Belmont Dairy, where you can now get more than milk to drink.

From Belmont, turn left on 33rd to Yamhill to an intersection painted by City Repair in a traffic calming, community-building project. Walk east on Yamhill to 38th; turn right and walk one block to Taylor. Turn left to return to the start.

Joan of Arc sculpture

Portland
Lloyd District and Sullivan's Gulch

This 1-mile walk explores the commercial areas of the Lloyd District and the quiet streets of Sullivan's Gulch, a neighborhood of classic Portland architecture. The walk begins at Holladay Park, a city park since 1870, where a spouting fountain and cast bronze sculptures invite walkers to soak in the city's ambience.

Begin at Holladay Park, NE Holladay Street and 11th Avenue. The park is named for Ben Holladay, who emigrated to California in 1856 at age 37 in search of his fortune. He found it there, organizing the country's largest stagecoach business. In 1866, he sold the business to Wells Fargo for $1.5 million. Two years later, fortune in hand, he arrived in Portland. By 1870, he had platted the Holladay subdivision and invested in a rail line down the east bank of the Willamette River. A big spender, Holladay over-extended himself and by 1876 he had lost the rail line.

Walk northeast through the park to the corner of 13th and Multnomah. Turn right on Multnomah and walk four blocks to 17th. Turn left, walk two blocks and turn right on Clackamas. Walk seven blocks through the Sullivan's Gulch neighborhood, part of Holladay's plat. From Clackamas, turn right on 24th, then right on Wasco. Walk on Wasco to 19th, turn left and then right on Multnomah to return to the park.

1.0 miles : **2112** steps : ▮▮▮▮ difficulty : ◈ 45.530, -122.653

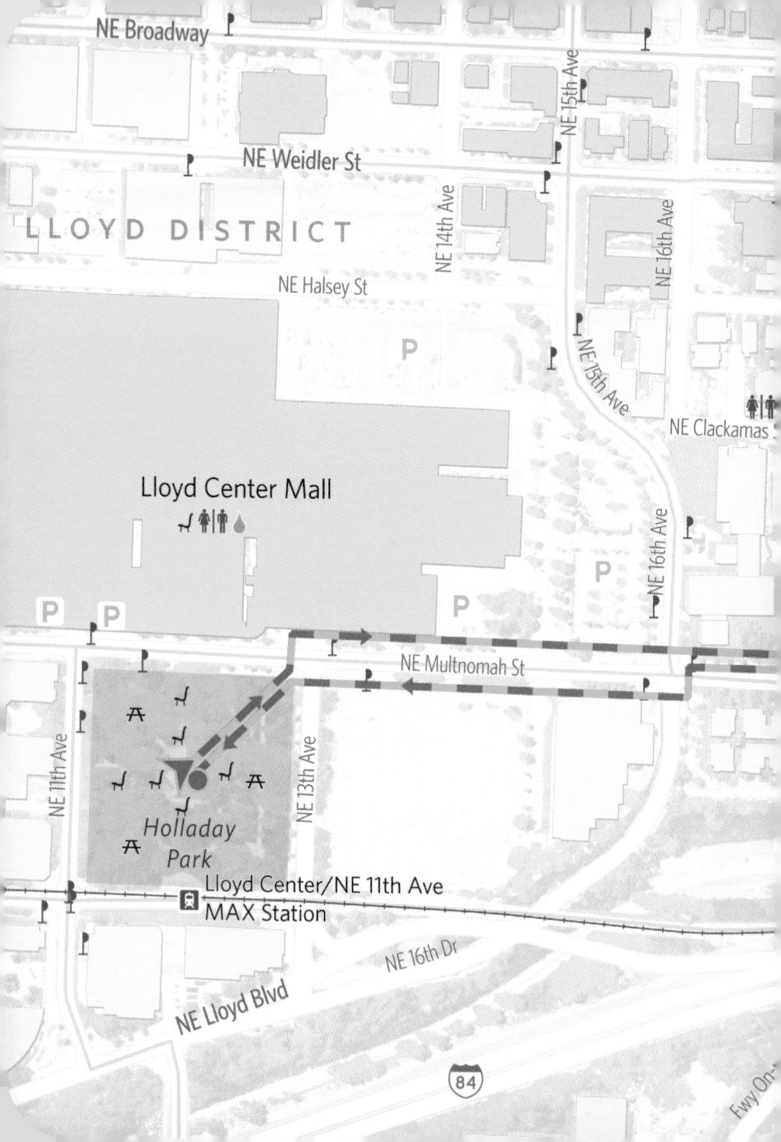

NE Broadway

NE 15th Ave

NE Weidler St

NE 14th Ave

LLOYD DISTRICT

NE 16th Ave

NE Halsey St

P

NE 13th Ave

NE Clackamas

Lloyd Center Mall

P

P

NE 16th Ave

P

P

P

NE Multnomah St

NE 11th Ave

NE 13th Ave

Holladay
Park

Lloyd Center/NE 11th Ave
MAX Station

NE 16th Dr

NE Lloyd Blvd

84

Fwy On

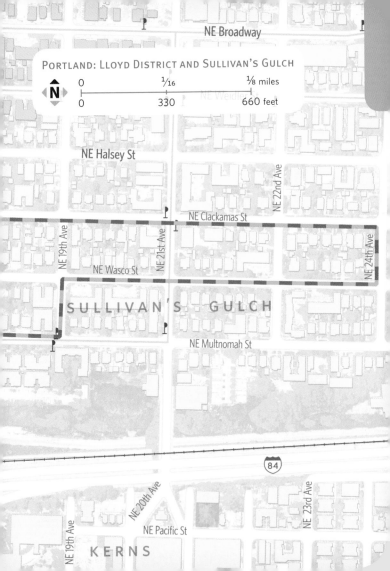

PORTLAND: LLOYD DISTRICT AND SULLIVAN'S GULCH

N

| 0 | | 1/16 | | 1/8 miles |
| 0 | | 330 | | 660 feet |

NE Broadway

NE Weidler St

NE Halsey St

NE 22nd Ave

NE Clackamas St

NE 19th Ave

NE 21st Ave

NE 24th Ave

NE Wasco St

SULLIVAN'S GULCH

NE Multnomah St

84

NE 20th Ave

NE 23rd Ave

NE Pacific St

NE 19th Ave

KERNS

The Lloyd Story

Located just north of Holladay Park, Lloyd Center Mall owes its origin to another man who made his fortune in California. An amateur geologist, Ralph B. Lloyd was convinced that oil lay below the surface of his Los Angeles area ranch. He was right. In 1920 he brought in the first of many gushers and spent his earnings buying what were then residential properties in Holladay's Addition, as Holladay's plat was called. The Sears-Roebuck store, now offices of Metro, was built on his property in 1929. In 1930 Lloyd Boulevard was named for him. Lloyd's further development plans, however, were interrupted by the Depression and World War II. Postwar, the Lloyd Corporation began a new development of the Lloyd District with demolition of old homes and construction of the Bonneville (Interior Department) Building. Lloyd Center Mall opened in 1960, at that time as an open-air mall. Lloyd had died seven years earlier.

● ● ●

Lloyd Center Mall

Portland
Mississippi and Overlook

In a 2-mile loop starting at beautiful, blufftop Overlook Park, walk a pedestrian bridge over I-5 to the vibrant neighborhood restaurants, shops and galleries along historic N Mississippi Avenue.

Begin at Overlook Park, at N Interstate Avenue and Fremont Street. Walk across Fremont to the east side of Interstate and begin walking north on Interstate. At Overlook Boulevard is the Kaiser Town Hall, a neighborhood meeting place named for nearby Kaiser Permanente, which first came to Overlook in 1959 with the Bess Kaiser Medical Center. Continue north. At Failing is St. Stanislaus Church, the heart of Portland's Polish community. From Interstate, turn right on Failing and cross the I-5 pedestrian bridge.

Once over the bridge, walk east on Failing two blocks to Mississippi. Turn right and shop and eat as you walk south, passing the ReBuilding Center at 3625, a project of the community-run Our United Villages. The center's donated inventory changes hourly, recycling an estimated 10 tons per day of construction waste; it is the largest nonprofit used building materials resource in North America.

From Mississippi, turn left on Fremont, then left on Albina. Walk two blocks to Failing, turn left and then right on Mississippi. At Skidmore is the John Palmer House, a spectacular 1898 Queen Anne home.

(continued on page 56)

2.1 miles | 4435 steps | difficulty | 45.547, -122.681

Beach Community Garden

N Going Ct

N Going St

N Prescott St

Patte Com Garc N Goi

5

N Prescott St MAX Station

N Skidmore St

N Maryland Ave

N Concord Ave

N Mason St

N Castle Ave

N Colonial Ave

N Massachusetts Ave

N Shaver St

N Montana Ave

N Missouri Ave

N Longview Ave

Overlook House Community Center

OVERLOOK

N Overlook Blvd

N Failing St

N Interstate Ave

N Melrose Dr

Overlook Park MAX Station

5

N Greeley Ave

Overlook Park

N Kaiser Center Dr

N Fremont St

PORTLAND: MISSISSIPPI AND OVERLOOK

N Blandena St

N Albina Ave

0   1/16   1/8 miles

0   330   660 feet

N Prescott St

N Commercial Ave

N Williams Ave

N Skidmore St

BOISE

N Mississippi Ave

N Mason St

N Gantenbein Ave

N Vancouver Ave

N Haight Ave

N Shaver St

N Albina Ave

N Kerby Ave

DeNorval
Unthank
Park

N Failing St

Jesuit
Volunteer
Community
Garden

N Borthwick Ave

N Commercial Ave

N Beech St

N Vancouver Ave

N Williams Ave

N Mississippi Ave

N Fremont St

Commercial Ave

Boise-Eliot
Community
Garden

N Ivy St

Boise-
Eliot ES

From Mississippi, turn left on Skidmore and walk west across I-5. At Interstate, turn left and return to the starting point at Overlook Park or take the MAX from the Prescott Station (just north of Skidmore) south to the station at Overlook Park.

A Look Back at Overlook

The Overlook area was home beginning in the late 1800s to Northern European immigrants who came to work in the Albina rail yards, which are visible below the bluff at Overlook Park. St. Stanislaus Church was built in 1907 by the area's many Polish immigrants, and the Kaiser Town Hall began life in the early 1900s as a Finnish lodge and social center. The light towers at the Overlook Park MAX station are reminiscent of roadside shrines in Poland. Each September, St. Stanislaus serves up 70,000 pierogis at its Polish Festival, the largest on the West Coast.

A Queen Anne home in Overlook

Portland
Pearl District and Nob Hill

Shopping, dining out, people-watching or attending the theater? Make an adventure of it and arrive by MAX or bus at PGE Park. From there, it's a short, fascinating walk through historic neighborhoods to shops, galleries, restaurants and theaters in the Pearl District or Nob Hill.

From the PGE Park MAX station, SW 18th Avenue and Morrison Street, walk north on 18th. PGE Park was once Multnomah Field, an athletic field built on the steep banks of Tanner Creek in 1893. PGE Park hosts Beavers baseball and Timbers soccer games.

At Burnside, 18th jogs right; continue north. At Everett, turn right, walk seven blocks, crossing I-405 and turn right on 11th. Walk to Couch. Here are the Brewery Blocks, redevelopment of land where Blitz-Weinhard brewed beer from 1856 to 1999. Today, you'll find Powell's Books, condominiums, restaurants, an upscale grocery, shops and Portland Center Stage's Gerding Theater in the smartly renovated Portland Armory building.

From 11th and Couch, walk east on Couch to Park Avenue and turn left to walk along the elm-lined North Park Blocks. At Glisan turn left, walk two blocks and turn right on 10th. From 10th, turn left on Johnson and left on 13th. Walk three blocks through the NW 13th Avenue National Historic District and turn right on Glisan. (Here you can return to the MAX by walking west on Glisan to 18th, turning left and walking south to the station.)

(continued on page 60)

3.3 miles : **6968** steps : **difficulty** : 45.522, -122.689

PORTLAND: PEARL DISTRICT AND NOB HILL

N

| 0 | 1/16 | 1/8 miles |
| 0 | 330 | 660 feet |

NW Thurman St

NW Savier St

30

NW Pettygrove St

405

NW Overton St

NW Northrup St

Tanner Springs Park

NW Lovejoy Ct

NW 16th Ave

NW 15th Ave

NW Station Way

NW Naito Pkwy

RTHWEST
ISTRICT

NW 17th Ave

Jamison Square

NW Johnson St

NW 9th Ave

NW Broadway

NW Irving St

NW 12th Ave

NW 11th Ave

NW 10th Ave

NW 13th Ave

NW Hoyt St

NW 18th Ave

Couch Park

NW Glisan St

NW 14th Ave

NW Flanders St

NW Park Ave

North Park Blocks

NW 19th Ave

NW Everett St

THE

NW 8th Ave

NW Trinity Pl

NW 17th Ave

NW Davis St

PEARL

NW Davis St

SW 19th Ave

NW Couch St

W Burnside St

Ankeny St

E Park

P

SW 17th Ave

SW 16th Ave

SW 15th Ave

SW 12th Ave

11th Ave

SW Alder S

SW Stark St

SW Oak St

Broadway

From 13th and Glisan, walk west on Glisan to 19th. Cross diagonally through Couch Park to Hoyt Street and continue west on Hoyt. Turn right on 23rd Avenue and enjoy blocks of shops and restaurants before turning left on Northrup. Walk three blocks and turn right on 26th. At Pettygrove, enter Wallace Park, where on September evenings hundreds gather to watch the world's largest population of Vaux's Swifts spiral into their home in Chapman School's tall chimney.

Exit the park and continue on 26th to Thurman. Turn right. At 23rd, a public library occupies a former wine store. Turn right on 23rd, walking south to Northrup. Go left and then right on 22nd. Walk three blocks; turn left at Kearney and right on 21st. Walk two blocks and turn left at Irving and right at 18th. Walk south on 18th to the starting point.

● ● ●

Vaux's Swifts sign

VAUX'S
SWIFTS

Swifts at Chapman School

Each September, thousands of Vaux's Swifts congregate in the chimney of Chapman Elementary School before they fly south for the winter. Just before dark, the swifts mass above Chapman School in a spiral formation and fly into

Portland
Pearl District to Pittock Mansion

This 2.8-mile one-way walk begins in the flats of Northwest Portland and gains over 800 feet as it climbs some of the city's longest staircases through Westover Heights, a neighborhood with spectacular Cascade Mountain views. It ends at Pittock Mansion, a restored French Renaissance Revival chateau. The home, its grounds, and its fabulous views are all open to the public.

Begin at NW 9th Avenue and Kearney Street. Walk west on Kearney, leaving the Pearl District as you pass under I-405. Continue west on Kearney to 24th, turn right and then left on Lovejoy. At 26th, keep right to walk on Cornell. Turn left at Summit Court and then left on Summit Avenue. On the right is a 160-step staircase. Take it to Westover Road; go right and continue across the intersection to Fairfax Terrace. There, go left up a 131-step staircase. At the top, continue straight on Cumberland and then left on Powhatan, and left on Warrenton Terrace. Keep to the left to follow Warrenton Terrace, turn right on Hermosa and right on Monte Vista Terrace; walk uphill on it, going around a gate to a pedestrian-only roadway that is part of the Pittock estate. Pass the home once occupied by the Pittock family's driver and continue up the roadway to the mansion. Views include the Columbia, Willamette, five Cascade peaks and downtown Portland.

On the return trip, NW 23rd and 21st avenues offer many places to eat and rest.

5.6 miles : 11827 steps : difficulty : 45.529, -122.680

NW Vaughn St
NW Vaughn St
NW Upshur St
NW 29th Ave
NW Thurman St
NW 26th Ave
NW Thurman St
NW Franklin Ct
NW 32nd Ave
NW 31st Ave
NW Thurman St
NW Savier St
NW 33rd Ave
NW 29th Ave
NW 28th Ave
NW 27th Ave
NW Savier St
NW Raleigh St
NW Raleigh St

NW 30th Ave
NW Quimby St
NW Quimby St
Chapman ES
Wallace Park
Forest Park
NW Cornell Rd
NW Pettygrove St

NW Summit Ave
NW Westover Rd
NW Cornell Rd
NW 26th Ave
NW 24th Ave

NW Luray Ter
NW Fairfax Ter
NW Shenandoah Ter
NW 25th Ave
NW Ma
NW Luray Circus
NW Wing Ln
NW Summit

NW Cumberland Rd
NW Culpepper Ter
NW Albemarle Ter
NW Kearney St
Greenbriar Ter
NW 24th Ave
Warrenton Ter
NW Powhatan Ter
Hillside Community Center
NW Ariel Ter
NW Macleay Blvd
NW Melinda Ave
NW Marlborough Ave
NW Westover Rd

Pittock Mansion and Acres
NW Rio Vista Ter
NW Macleay Blvd
NW Alpine Ter
N W Macleay Blvd
Roanoke St
NW Mildred St
Pittock Dr
NW Valle Vista Ter
NW Hermosa Blvd
NW Monte Vista Ter
Rainier Ter
Lomita Ter
Beulah Vista Ter
NW Mildred St
NW Uptown Ter
NW 24th Pl

NW Verde Vista Ter
NW Santanita Ter
NW Imperial Ter
NW Calumet Ter
NW Macleay Blvd
NW Maywood Dr
SW Tichner Dr
SW Wright Ave
SW Washington Way

Hoyt Arboretum
NW Hermosa Blvd
W Burnside Rd
SW Champlain Dr
SW Radon Ave
SW Livingston Ter
Marconi Ave
Washington Park

PORTLAND: PEARL DISTRICT TO PITTOCK...

N

0   ⅛   ¼ miles

0   660   1320 feet

The Pittock Story

At 75 years old, Henry Pittock, with his wife Georgina, commissioned architect Edward Foulkes to design their retirement home. Construction took five years and cost $350,000 by the home's completion in 1914.

Pittock, publisher of the Oregonian from 1860 to his death in 1919, loved gadgets. Inside is an Otis elevator, intercom, central vacuum system and walk-in freezer. He was also an avid outdoorsman who carved many of the trails in the woods near the mansion.

The last family member, a grandson, moved out of the mansion in 1958. The home was for sale when the 1962 Columbus Day storm severely damaged it. Demolition appeared likely until a group of citizen activists stepped up and worked with the City of Portland to save the home. In 1964, for $225,000, the City purchased the mansion and grounds. It has since been impeccably restored.

● ● ●

Pittock Mansion

Portland
Peninsula Park and 4 Neighborhoods

This 2.6-mile loop begins at a landmark Multnomah County library, and passes through Piedmont, a beautiful streetcar-era neighborhood, before heading back along Interstate Avenue and the busy scene at Portland Community College's Cascade Campus.

Begin at the North Portland Library, N Killingsworth Street and Commercial Avenue. Cross Killingsworth and head north on Commercial. Turn left at Jessup and right at Kerby. Cross Ainsworth at the pedestrian crossing and enter Peninsula Park. From the sunken rose gardens, walk north along the gravel path that becomes paved toward the community center.

Leave the park at its northwest corner, Albina and Rosa Parks Way. Cross Rosa Parks Way at the light and turn right. In one block, turn left onto Borthwick; north of Dekum, pass the redevelopment of the former Villa St. Rose, once a Catholic convent and girls school, now an award-winning housing development.

From Borthwick turn left on Bryant and continue west to the wall for I-5. Turn left on a path and then right to cross the freeway on a pedestrian bridge. Once across, turn left on a frontage path and then right on Saratoga. Walk west to Interstate Avenue and turn left, walking 12 blocks to Killingsworth (or take the MAX from the Rosa Parks Way station to the Killingsworth station). Turn left on Killingsworth, walking east on its north side. At Albina, cross to the south side of Killingsworth and walk to the starting point.

2.6 miles : **5548** steps : ◧▮▮ difficulty : ◈ 45.562, -122.671

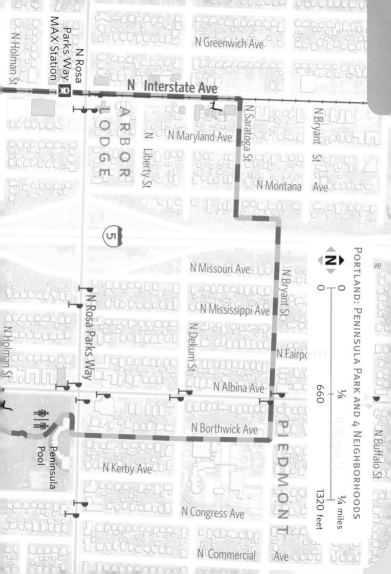

PORTLAND: PENINSULA PARK AND 4 NEIGHBORHOODS

N

N Holman St
N Rosa Parks Way MAX Station
N Greenwich Ave
N Interstate Ave
N Maryland Ave
N Saratoga St
N Bryant St
ARBOR LODGE
N Liberty St
N Montana Ave
5
N Missouri Ave
N Bryant St
N Mississippi Ave
N Dekum St
N Fairport Pl
N Rosa Parks Way
N Holman St
N Albina Ave
N Borthwick Ave
PIEDMONT
Peninsula Pool
N Kerby Ave
N Congress Ave
N Commercial Ave
N Buffalo St

0   660   1320 feet
0   ⅛   ¼ miles

Peninsula Park

Peninsula Park's land was once owned by a local businesswoman known as Liverpool Liz who operated a roadhouse and horse racetrack. The park, completed in 1913, retains many of its original features, including a community center (the city's oldest), lantern-style streetlights, stone pillars, brickwork and the nearly century old fountain in the center of the rose garden. The 2-acre garden, the only sunken rose garden in Oregon, is formally planted with 8,900 roses. The official Portland rose, Mme. Caroline Testout, is here, a rose once planted by the thousands along city streets. The octagonal bandstand overlooking the rose garden was constructed in 1913. It is now on the National Register of Historic Places; in World War I, patriotic demonstrations were held there; today it is the scene of summer weddings and concerts.

Mme. Caroline Testout, the official Portland rose

Portland
Swan Island Beach

Walk on the beach...on Swan Island? It's true. Swan Island beaches offer close-ups of resident geese and osprey and the occasional bald eagle, beaver and even river otter. And where else can you find great views of a real working harbor: active docks and shipbuilding, all with Portland's downtown skyline as backdrop?

Begin this 2.2-mile (one-way) walk at the Prescott Street MAX Station on N Interstate Avenue. Walk one block north on Interstate, cross to the north side of Going Street and head west, downhill. Pass under Greeley Avenue, then over the Union Pacific train tracks.

Cross Basin Avenue on the marked crosswalk and pass signs welcoming you to "Port of Portland's Swan Island Industrial Park." Swan Island was once a true island, with the Willamette's main channel on its east side. Its S curve as the river hit the bluff was a navigation hazard, so the current channel was dredged in the 1920s. Adjoining wetlands disappeared under fill and the island became a peninsula joined to the mainland with a causeway.

Cross Port Center Way and Going Street at the light, by a McDonald's; head straight toward the river via the sidewalk and then right on the access trail adjacent the Swan Island Pump Station, the heart of Portland's $1.4 billion effort to keep untreated sewage out of the river.

At the river, turn left, walking upriver on the North Portland Greenway Trail, planned to ultimately connect the St. Johns Bridge with

(continued on page 72)

4.4 miles : 9292 steps : difficulty : 45.555, -122.682

N Emerson St

N Basin Ave

N Webster St

N Commerce St

N Lagoon Ave

N Emerson St

N Channel Ave

N Ballast St

N Anchor St

N Wygant St

N Basin Ave

P

North Portland Greenway Trail

N Channel Ave

McCarthy Park

Ports O' Call building

N Port Center Way

Willamette

River

NW Front Ave

PORTLAND: SWAN ISLAND BEACH

N

0	⅛	¼ miles
0	660	1320 feet

the Eastbank Esplanade. At tall cottonwoods, the trail ends. Turn around and walk downstream; beach access is on the left. Pass office buildings for Freightliner, Swan Island's largest employer. Continue along the river to the arched footbridge at the Ports O' Call building. Here, the trail ends. Reverse direction and turn left onto the access trail and back out to the parking access road. Go left to walk on the sidewalk in front of the Ports O' Call building. It leads to the riverside McCarthy Park. From here, walk north on the Greenway Trail about 0.5 mile.

To return, retrace your steps to the MAX stop. Or, to catch a bus, walk a block inland from McCarthy Park to the TriMet stop 72, with frequent service to the Killingsworth Avenue MAX station.

● ● ●

Overlooking Portland's waterfront

East Region

	D	N	P	C	H	L
A. Gresham: Butler Creek Greenway Trail p. 75	2.2	•				
B. Gresham: Downtown p. 79	1.6			•	•	•
C. Gresham: Gresham Butte Saddle Trail p. 85	3.7	•	•	•	•	
D. Gresham: Springwater Corridor Trail p. 89	5.2	•		•	•	•
E. Troutdale: Downtown and Parks p. 93	2.4	•		•	•	•
F. Clackamas Co.: Mount Talbert Nature Park p. 97	4.0	•	•			
G. Milwaukie/Oak Grove: Trolley Trail p. 101	7.8	•	•	•	•	
H. Milwaukie: Downtown and Riverfront p. 107	2.4	•		•	•	•
I. Portland: Ardenwald and Johnson Creek p. 111	2.5	•			•	•
J. Portland: Brooklyn and Rail Yards p. 115	3.2			•	•	
K. Portland: Southeast Creeks and Bridges p. 119	4.6	•	•	•		
L. Portland: Colonial Heights and Ladd's ... p. 123	2.3			•	•	•
M. Portland: Sellwood and Oaks Bottom p. 127	3.8	•				
N. Portland: Westmoreland to Crystal Springs p. 131	4.0	•		•		•
O. Portland: Mount Tabor p. 135	2.1	•	•		•	

D   Distance in Miles   C   City Cruise

N   Nature Walk   H   History Walk

P   Power Walk   L   Lunchtime Stroll

Gresham
Butler Creek Greenway Trail

This short loop travels along the Butler Creek Greenway Trail, passing Binford Lake and a neighborhood park before looping back on neighborhood streets to a pedestrian bridge over Johnson Creek. From there, walking options are wide-ranging, as you access the Springwater Corridor Trail that runs from Portland to Boring.

Start on 14th Drive at Binford Avenue. Head west on 14th approximately 75 feet and turn left onto the Butler Creek Greenway Trail. Head south on it, crossing Binford Lake Parkway. On the left is Binford Lake. Continue south along the lake through a greenway open space, following Butler Creek. The trail then enters Butler Creek Park, where a loop trail leads in either direction.

Leave the south end of the park at 27th Drive near Mawrcrest Avenue, turn left on 27th and then left onto Wonderview Drive. Cross Binford Lake Parkway, where Wonderview changes name to Heiney Road. Continue north on Heiney; it turns west and changes name to 14th Drive. Continue west past the walk's start point and turn right off 14th to a scenic viewpoint of Johnson Creek and the 135-foot-long pedestrian bridge over the creek. Return to the starting point by retracing your steps to 14th Drive.

For a longer walk, at the pedestrian bridge over Johnson Creek, continue north 0.25 mile to the Springwater Corridor Trail. Walk 1.5 miles east to historic downtown Gresham or 1.7 miles west to Powell Butte Nature Park.

2.2 miles   **4646** steps   ▊▊▊▊ difficulty   ◈ 45.486, -122.460

SE 190th Dr

SW Sandlewood Ln

GRESHAM: BUTLER CREEK GREENWAY TRAIL

N

0   0
      ⅛
660

¼
1320 feet

½ miles

SW 33rd St

SW B

SW

SW 28th Ct

SW 30th St

SW Tegart Ave

SW Brixton Ave

SW Meyers Pl

SW Battaglia Ave

SW Mawrcrest Ave

SW Lillyben Ave

SW Willow Pkwy

SW 30th Dr

SW 33rd St

SW 24th Ter

SW 25th Ct

SW 26th St

SW Redfern

SW Tegart Ave

SW Brixton Dr

SW Eastwood Ave

SW 23rd St

SW Willow Pky

SW 28th Ct

SW 26th Ct

SW 25th Ct

SW Meyers Dr

SW 24th St

Butler

SW 22nd Ct

Butler Creek Park

SW Battaglia Pl

SW Eleven Mile Dr

SW 27th Dr

SW 26th St

SW 24th St

SW 23rd St

SW Lillyben Ct

SW 29th Dr

SW 26th Ct

SW 25th St

SW Wonderview Dr

SW 24th

Butler Creek Park

Butler Creek Park is a 4-acre neighborhood park with a play area, picnic tables, basketball court and wheelchair accessible areas. Butler Creek, a tributary of Johnson Creek, has been impounded to form Binford Lake, where birdlife abounds.

From the Springwater Corridor Trail access at the end of this walk, you can walk 1.7 miles west to 570 acre Powell Butte Nature Park. Its 9 miles of trails invite mountain bikers, hikers and horseback riders to explore this volcanic butte, with its forests of bigleaf maple, Douglas fir and Pacific dogwood. Also in the park are rolling meadows and orchards from long-ago farms. Wildlife abounds.

● ● ●

Great Egret

Gresham
Downtown

1.6 miles : 3377 steps : difficulty : ◈ 45.502, -122.426

Gresham was named in 1884 after U.S. Postmaster General Walter Quinton Gresham. Since then the small community on the banks of Johnson Creek has grown to Oregon's fourth largest city. This walk explores its revitalized downtown and MAX connections. With MAX access and portals to the Springwater Corridor Trail, Gresham is an easy place to explore while leaving your car at home.

Begin at the Cleveland Avenue MAX Station near Liberty Avenue. Walk on the north side of the MAX tracks west toward Cleveland Avenue. Look across the tracks to the Chestnut Lane Assisted Living Community, which serves deaf and deaf-blind individuals from across the United States. Turn right on Cleveland and then left on 8th. Walk west on 8th, passing Alpha High School, an alternative school that offers a school-to-work curriculum; Cedar Neighborhood Park; and the East County Health, Aging and Disability Service Center, home to the Community Senior Center and Loaves and Fishes.

Continue west on 8th through the Gresham Central Transit Center. Cross Hood Avenue, heading south (left) on Hood. Cross 10th Drive and the MAX tracks and then turn right onto the promenade that runs parallel and south of the tracks. The promenade is a joint project of TriMet, which donated the land; the City of Gresham, which maintains the facilities; and the Gresham Central Apartments, which maintains the grass, sweeps the walks and empties trash cans. From the promenade, turn left on Roberts, right on 5th Street and left on Main.

Like many commercial centers along the MAX line, Gresham's downtown is a place where people live, work and recreate without getting into a car. The Historic Downtown Plan has been in effect since 1993, revitalizing a downtown that had languished post World War II, but is now revived with shops, restaurants, housing and parks. The plan changed zoning to encourage mixed-use development, pedestrian friendly buildings and a strong orientation to the light rail line and bus transit. Old storefronts commingle with newer buildings. Don't miss the Gresham Pioneer Museum at 410 N. Main, housed in an old Carnegie library that was superseded in 1990 by the new library, a few blocks away at 385 NW Miller Ave.

From Main, turn left onto Powell Boulevard; as you walk one block, you skirt the northern edge of Main City Park, a large park bordering Johnson Creek. The land was once called Camp Ground, after the Portland Methodists' use of the land for meetings in the 1880s.

From Powell, turn left onto Roberts Avenue, right on 3rd and left on Hood. Here is visible the future site of the Center for the Arts, at the southeast corner of 3rd and Hood. A Pedestrian Plaza will be home to outdoor events. Continue north on Hood, cross the MAX tracks and turn right on 10th to end at the Central Transit Center. Here is an open air concrete living room created by Mount Hood Community College art students, a great place to relax after your walk.

Gresham at night

NW 8th St

NW Earl Ave

NE 10th Dr

The Promenade

NE 8th St

Kelly Ave

Gresham TC

NE

Gresham
Central TC
MAX Station

NE 7th St

NE Roberts Ave

NE Hood Ave

NW 5th St

NW Miller Ave

Gresham
Pioneer
Museum

NE 4th St

NE Beech Ave

NE 4th St

N Main Ave

NW 3rd St

GRESHAM

NE Hood Ave

NE 3rd St

NE 2nd St

Cultural Arts
Center Site

NE Kelly Ave

NE 2nd St

NW 1st St

NE Roberts Ave

E Powell Blvd

S Main Ave

Main City
Park

SE Hood Ave

SE Kelly Ave

NE 9th St

Cedar
Neighborhood
Park

NE Linden Ave

NE 8th St

Ave

Cleveland

P

Cleveland
Ave MAX
Station

NE 6th St

NE

NE Linden Ave

Ave

NE 5th St

NE Liberty Ave

NE 4th St

NE Elliott Ave

NE Linden Ave

NE Juniper Ave

NE 3rd St

NE 2nd St

GRESHAM: DOWNTOWN

◀ **N** ▶

0	¹/₁₆	⅛ miles
0	330	660 feet

E Powell Blvd

SE Juniper Ave

SE 1st St

Linden Ave

SE Cleveland Ave

A Rich Rail History

Parts of the Eastside MAX line travel the same right of way as the Mount Hood Railway and Power Company interurban rail line, which ran between Northeast Portland's Montavilla neighborhood and Bull Run, east of Sandy.

The old interurban right of way is used by the MAX between 99th Avenue and Burnside in Portland to Gresham's Cleveland MAX Station. Diesel freight service continued on the line through Gresham into the 1980s, when it was converted to a right of way for the MAX. The MAX opened in 1986 after four years of construction. The MAX Blue Line to Portland was one of the first modern light rail systems in the nation and began our region's shift toward innovative land-use and transportation planning.

To view Gresham's Significant Trees, stop at Gresham City Hall (1333 NW Eastman Parkway) to pick up a brochure in the Department of Environmental Services. Hours are 8 a.m. to 5 p.m.

● ● ●

MAX in Gresham

Gresham
Gresham Butte Saddle Trail

After a hike through Gresham's largest natural area with its mature forest and abundance of wildlife, this walk follows the Springwater Corridor Trail through the original Gresham town site and by three wooded cemeteries where Gresham's pioneers are buried.

Begin at the dead-end of 19th Drive off Towle Avenue. Walk east 1.25 miles through the Gresham Butte Natural Area along old logging roads. Volunteers have cleared out non-native species and planted salal, sword fern and vine maple.

Leave the trail at Meadow Court at 19th Street. Walk to 19th and turn left, following 19th to Regner Road. Turn left on Regner, following it to its intersection with the Springwater Corridor Trail. Turn left and walk along the trail. It intersects Main Avenue in Main City Park, the site of the original town that developed around Johnson Creek. For a side trip to historic downtown Gresham, turn right on Main and cross Powell Boulevard where you'll find restaurants and shops.

Continue on the Springwater Trail to Walters Road. Here, along the banks of Johnson Creek are pioneer cemeteries – Gresham Pioneer Cemetery, founded in 1859; and Escobar Cemetery, founded in 1914. The White Birch Cemetery, on the west side of Walters Road, was founded in 1888. From the cemeteries, continue on the trail to Towle Road. Exit the trail and walk south on Towle to 19th Drive. Turn left on 19th to return to the starting point.

3.7 miles | **7814** steps | difficulty | 45.483, -122.447

GRESHAM: GRESHAM BUTTE SADDLE TRAIL

N

| 0 | | ⅛ | | ¼ miles |
| 0 | 660 | | 1320 feet |

SW 1st Ct

SW 1st Ct

SW Florence Ave

SW Eastman Pkwy

SW Wonderview Dr

SW Wonderview Dr

SW Willow

SW 4th St

SW 3rd Dr

SW 5th Pl

SW 4th St

SW Angeline Ave

SW 6th Pl

SW 5th St

SW Birdsdale Dr

SW 5th Ct

Johnson Creek

SW 4th St

SW 5th Ave

SW Day Ct

SW Sleret Ave

SW Wilson Ct

SW Overlook Ct

SW Blaine

Hollybrook
Neighborhood
Park

Hollydale
ES

SW 7th Ct

Angeline Ave

SW Florence Ave

8th St

SW 7th Ct

SW Clara Drd MS

SW 8th Dr

SW 8th Dr

SW

Pl

Springwater Corridor

SW 10th Ct

SW 10th Dr

SW Florence Ct

Gresham

SW 10th Ct

SW Chastain Dr

Butte

Natural

Area

SW 13th Ct SW 13th St

SW 14th St

Walters Hill

SW Wallula Dr

SW Willowbrook Ave

SW 15th St

SW Orchard Ave

SW Towle Ave

SW Walters

SW Blaine

SW Blaine Ct

Loop

SW 17th St

SW 17th Ct

SW 18th St

SW 19th Dr

SW Angeline Ave

SW Chastain Ave

SW 20th Ct

SW 20th Ct

SW 21st Ter

ew

Ave

SW 22nd Ter

SW 23rd Ter

Gresham Trivia

Gresham's many buttes are Boring Lava domes, formations created from eruptions that occurred between 100,000 and 6,000,000 years ago as the Portland Basin was pulled apart by tectonic forces. Rocky Butte and Mount Tabor in Portland are also Boring Lava domes.

In Gresham Pioneer Cemetery is the grave of Miyo Iwakoshi, believed to be the first Japanese person to live in Oregon. She and her Scottish husband built a sawmill east of Gresham and named the new settlement Orient, to honor her heritage. Orient exists today. Gresham's pioneer cemeteries are managed by Metro as active facilities. Public inquiries are welcome concerning gravesite selection, and other services. Metro also maintains burial records for use by family historians and genealogists. Visit www.oregonmetro.gov/cemeteries for more information.

Gresham Pioneer Cemetery

Gresham
Springwater Corridor Trail

These two walks travel part of the 16.8-mile Springwater Corridor Trail, the first urban Rails-to-Trails conversion project in Oregon. It runs from near the Willamette River in Portland to Boring, Oregon. Along Gresham's 4.8 miles of the trail, pass restored railroad trestles and wetlands, and visit sites of Gresham's history. The trail roughly parallels Johnson Creek, one of the last free-flowing streams in the metro area.

Route One

[**5.2** miles **10982** steps ▥▥▥ difficulty ◈ 45.495, -122.430]

The first route, a 2.6-mile one-way walk, heads west from downtown Gresham. Enter the Springwater Corridor Trail at 219 S. Main Avenue in Main City Park. At Walters Drive, investigate three pioneer cemeteries adjacent to the trail. Continue west on the trail to Linneman Station, a replica of a 1903 streetcar station that burned down at this site in 1995. The station, once a popular destination for weekend tourists from Portland, is one of the last remaining depots in Oregon's once-extensive interurban electric railway system. It features railroad memorabilia and artifacts of early Gresham life.

From Linneman Station, continue west; turn right on Highland Drive and walk about 0.25 mile on the sidewalk to Powell Boulevard. Turn right on Powell to catch Bus 9 east back to Gresham Central Station. To travel west to Portland, cross Powell at Highland, turn left and walk 350 feet to the bus stop. Or return to the start by retracing your steps.

(continued on page 92)

GRESHAM: SPRINGWATER CORRIDOR TRAIL

N

| 0 | ¼ | ½ miles |
| 0 | 1320 | 2640 feet |

Route Two

[**4.0** miles **8448** steps ▮▮▮▮ difficulty ✦ 45.495, -122.430]

The second route, 2 miles one-way, heads east from downtown Gresham. Enter the Springwater Trail at Main City Park and head southeast, passing the Hogan Road trailhead at 1.3 miles. Continue another 0.25 mile; on the right is the historic Ambleside area. At the turn of the last century, many prominent Portland families had summer homes in Ambleside, a planned community designed around a series of ponds, waterfalls, rock walls and footpaths, with Johnson Creek meandering through the center.

About 250 feet further on the trail and to the left is the Columbia Brick Works Company, founded in 1906 by Franz Olbrich. One of 68 brickyards in the Portland area at that time, it produced more than 150 varieties of bricks. Now it is one of only two brick factories still operating in Oregon. Interpretive signage describes the history of the site.

Continue southeast on the trail to Palmblad Road. Retrace your steps to the start.

● ● ●

Joggers on the Springwater Corridor Trail

Troutdale
Downtown and Parks

This 1.2-mile one-way walk connects picturesque down-town Troutdale with its historic rail depot and pioneer home to the riverside Glenn Otto Park and Lewis and Clark State Park. Both parks offer trails and access to the Sandy River.

From the intersection of SW 257th Avenue and East Columbia River Highway, walk east along the historic highway on sidewalks through downtown Troutdale. At the northeastern end of down-town is the Depot Rail Museum and Depot Park, site of the town's 1907 train depot. From Depot Park, cross the highway and follow the walkway south approximately 0.25 mile to the Harlow House Park and Barn Museum. From the Harlow House, continue south, following the road as it turns east, crosses Beaver Creek and enters Glenn Otto Park. From the park, follow the highway bike lane east over the Sandy River via the historic Troutdale Bridge. On the east end of the bridge, turn north (left) and walk 0.25 mile to Lewis and Clark State Recreation Site and Broughten's Bluff, the westernmost point in the Columbia River Gorge. Interpretive displays in the park describe its history. Retrace your steps to return to the start.

2.4 miles · **5069** steps · ▟▙ difficulty · ◈ 45.540, -122.390

TROUTDALE: DOWNTOWN AND PARKS

N

| 0 | 1/16 | 1/8 miles |
| 0 | 330 | 660 feet |

NW Graham Road

Columbia River Hwy

E Columbia River Hwy

De
P

Mayor's
Square

SW 257th Dr

SW Kendall St

SW 2nd St

SW

S Buxton Rd

SE Dora St

SE Harlow Ave

SE Kibling St

SE 2nd St

SE

SE 3rd St

TROUTDALE

SW 4th St

SE 4th St

SE Kibling St

SE 5th St

SE Sandy Ave

Helen
Althaus
Park

SE 6th St

Troutdale ES

Strawbe
Meado
Greenw

SW 7th St

SE 7th St

SE Sandy Ave

th Cir

Martine
Ct

SE 8th St

SW

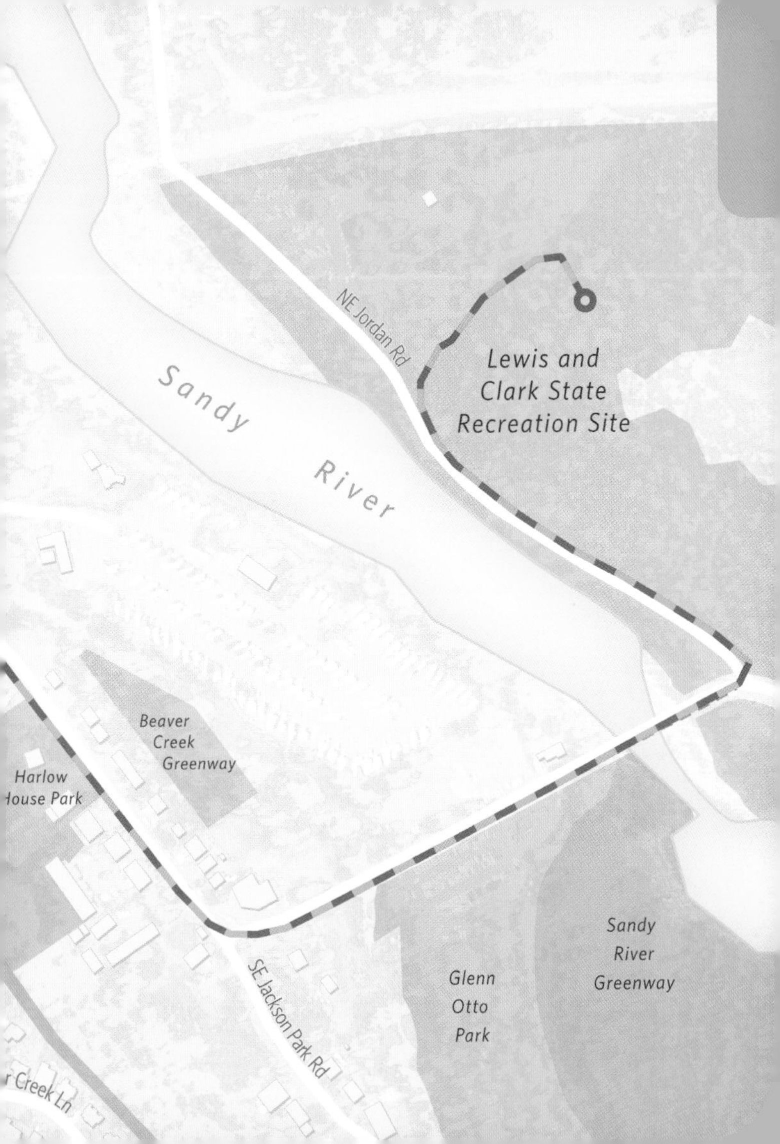

Lewis and
Clark State
Recreation Site

NE Jordan Rd

Sandy

River

Beaver
Creek
Greenway

Harlow
House Park

SE Jackson Park Rd

Sandy
River
Greenway

Glenn
Otto
Park

r Creek Ln

The Troutdale Story

Many of the shops and businesses in downtown Troutdale have been rebuilt to reflect a turn of the century feel. The Harlow House was built in 1900 by the son of Captain John Harlow. Captain Harlow, the founder of Troutdale, created trout ponds in the vicinity of the Harlow House; it was from these ponds the town derived its name.

Glenn Otto Park was named after a town mayor. The park is on the banks of the Sandy River and offers numerous picnic sites and easy river access. The Troutdale Bridge crossing the Sandy was constructed in 1912 by Multnomah County for $20,000.

Lewis and Clark State Park commemorates the Lewis and Clark expedition and their exploration of the Sandy River in 1805. Broughton's Bluff in the park is named for Lt. William Robert Broughton who navigated the Columbia in 1792 to the mouth of the Sandy and is responsible for the naming of Mount Hood. Day hikers and technical rock climbers will find bluff trails and rock formations provide a challenge and great view from the top.

● ● ●

Downtown Troutdale

Clackamas County
Mount Talbert Nature Park

Mount Talbert is an extinct volcanic butte, similar to other Boring Lava domes in the Portland area such as Mount Tabor or Rocky Butte. With a series of loop trails, you can explore the varied landscapes of the metro region's newest protected natural area.

Note: dogs and bikes are not permitted.

The walk begins at the trailhead to the Mount Talbert Nature Park, at 10695 SE Mather Road, south of Sunnyside Road. Here, access 4.0 miles of loop trails that travel through Douglas fir forest, along streams and through oak woodlands and upland prairies. Some firs are being girdled, a practice that kills them so that the slower growing native Oregon white oaks can thrive. Interpretive signs provide information about the plants and animals that can be seen – and heard – at the nature park.

Non-human residents and visitors to Mount Talbert include deer, coyote, raccoon, Western gray squirrel, rubber boa, pileated and hairy woodpecker, white-breasted nuthatch, Western tanager and many more. Birds and birders like Mount Talbert's "edges," its many transition areas between forests and open meadows, old farmsteads and apple orchards. Bring binoculars and watch out for poison oak along the trail.

Near the 750-foot summit, views of downtown Portland, the metro area and Cascade Mountain peaks can be seen through the tree canopy.

4.0 miles : **8448** steps : |||| difficulty : ◀◈▶ 45.420, -122.553

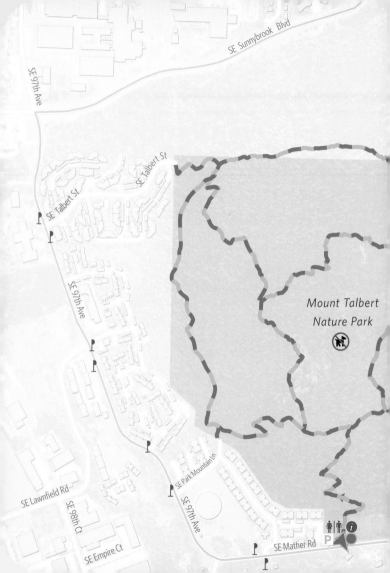

SE Sunnybrook Blvd

SE 97th Ave

SE Talbert St

SE Talbert St

SE 97th Ave

Mount Talbert
Nature Park

SE Park Mountain Ln

SE Lawnfield Rd

SE 98th Ct

SE 97th Ave

SE Empire Ct

SE Mather Rd

SE Timber Valley Dr

SE 117th

SE Sunnyside Rd

SE Forest Creek Ct

SE 118th Dr

SE Market Dr

SE 119th Dr

SE 122nd Ave

SE Sunnycreek Ln

SE Idyllwild Ct

Sunnycreek
Open Space

SE Hidalgo Ct

SE Cedar Park Dr

SE Warren Ct

SE 119th Ct

SE Melbrook Way

SE 121st Pl

SE Mather Rd

SE 116th Ct

SE 119th Dr

SE 120th Way

SE Tawny Dr

SE Willingham Ct

SE Mather Rd

SE 115th Ave

SE Abby Ln

SE Falbrook Dr

SE 122nd Ave

SE Summer Pl

SE Cra...

ns Ct

CLACKAMAS COUNTY: MOUNT TALBERT NATURE PARK

Ashley St

N

0	⅛	¼ miles
0	660	1320 feet

SE Meadows

SE 116

New Park Links Neighbors to Nature

Surrounded by neighborhoods, Mount Talbert is one of the last large undeveloped natural areas in the metro region. The butte was protected by Metro and the North Clackamas Parks and Recreation District with funds from a voter approved bond measure. The park, opened officially in 2007, offers hiking trails and information about its cultural and natural resources. Parts of the site are being restored as upland prairie and oak savannah, an ecosystem that once covered 500,000 acres in the Willamette Valley. Today only 1 percent of the valley's indigenous oak savannah habitat remains. Much of it has been converted to agricultural use.

Many park trails were built over the years by volunteers – neighbors living at the base of the butte. The nature park includes the summit of the butte as well as west-facing slopes visible to the tens of thousands who travel I-205 every day.

● ● ●

White oak

Milwaukie/Oak Grove
Trolley Trail

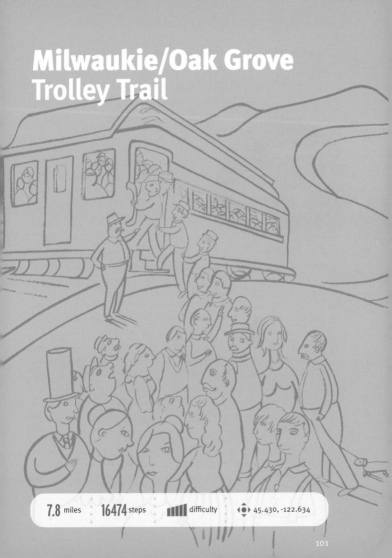

7.8 miles : **16474** steps : **difficulty** : 45.430, -122.634

Running from Milwaukie to Gladstone, the Trolley Trail is a walk through the past. This 3.9 mile (one-way) walk follows part of the route of the Oregon City Line, a Portland Traction Company interurban streetcar line that once ran between Portland and Oregon City.

Trolley at Evergreen Station

Before 1893, residents of the Milwaukie area relied on dirt roads; travel was by foot, horse-drawn wagon or, least arduously, the Willamette River on the town's west edge. In 1893, the trolley came to town and changed life for Milwaukie residents; this trail explores part of its length.

Begin at SE McLoughlin Boulevard and Park Avenue. From Park turn left on 27th, where you will see an entrance to the Trolley Trail.

Walk south on the trail and pass Oak Grove Elementary School. Once the trail becomes Arista Drive, cross Courtney Avenue. The streetcar stop Courtney Station, named for an Irish chicken farmer, was at the southwest corner of Arista and Courtney. Continue south on Arista. At Pine Avenue, a large evergreen hedge once marked the boundary for the Little Flower sanitarium. Saint Theresa Station, named for the sanitarium's patron saint, was on the east side of Arista between Courtney and Oak Grove Boulevard. At Oak Grove Boulevard was another station which doubled as a general store. It now houses the Oak Grove Bar and Grill.

By the 1920s, streetcar travel reached a peak it would never see again, as automobiles began to change the landscape and the Great Depression soon would slow economic activity. Ridership rose again during

World War II, as workers at Portland's wartime shipyards were encouraged to use public transit to save gasoline needed for the war effort.

Continue south on Arista and north of Creighton Avenue watch for the trail to veer left through vegetation. The trail travels close to several residences, emerges at Rupert Drive, and continues along a grassy median between the upper and lower portions of Arista. The trolley tracks reveal themselves in places here. Cross Concord Road and continue on the trail, traveling close to homes and through wooded areas.

Beyond Roethe Road, the trail travels near homes and industrial land to Boardman Avenue. Cross Boardman and walk on Arista. The trolley alignment runs along a raised berm, but stay on Arista to where it merges with McLoughlin. Walk south on McLoughlin, crossing to its other side at the four-way stop at Jennings Avenue. South of Jennings, watch immediately for a small, inconspicuous left onto Abernethy Lane. Walk south on Abernethy, cross Meldrum Avenue and the trail ends at Glen Echo Avenue.

Older days in Oak Grove

Retrace your steps to the starting point.

From Trolley to Trail

The remote, small-town character of Milwaukie changed when a streetcar line to Portland was built in 1893 by the Oregon City and Southern Railway. Passenger service along the line meant that bedroom communities sprang up, with workers commuting into Portland. The rail line was taken over in 1901 by what would eventually become Portland General Electric. It operated the line as the Portland Traction Company starting in 1930.

In 1958, with automobiles having supplanted interurban lines in the Portland area, passenger service stopped. Freight service continued until 1968, when the line was abandoned. In that year, a local high school teacher initiated a campaign to preserve the corridor as a trail. Three decades later, efforts by citizens and officials to keep the right of way open to the public ended happily. In 2001, Metro and the North Clackamas Parks and Recreation District purchased the right of way with plans to turn it into a multiuse trail.

● ● ●

At the Oak Grove Station

Milwaukie
Downtown and Riverfront

Milwaukie is one of the oldest towns on the Willamette River, at one time rivaling Portland as the pre-eminent local port. On this walk, you'll discover Milwaukie's connections to the river, see its historic downtown and glimpse where the city is heading in the future.

Begin at SE Harrison and Main streets at Milwaukie's City Hall. Walk east on Harrison, passing the Ledding Library and also a Waldorf School, constructed in 1937 as a WPA project. From Harrison, turn right on 28th and then right on Washington. Walk west; after crossing McLoughlin, enter Riverfront Park and continue straight to the Kellogg Creek Trail. Walk on the asphalt path along the river.

Walk south on this trail 0.2 mile to Eagle Street and 19th Avenue. Stay straight on 19th to Spring Park's entrance at Sparrow Street. Take the hiking trail from the entrance 0.2 mile as it winds around the south side of a bay from which Elk Rock Island is visible.

To return, walk north on 19th to the Kellogg Creek Trail at Riverfront Park. Walk straight (north) on the trail and cross the bridge near Washington Street. Continue north to Monroe. Turn right on Monroe, cross McLoughlin and turn left on Main. At Main and Monroe, pass Dark Horse Comics, one of the nation's largest comic book publishers. Walk one block north to the intersection of Harrison and Main.

2.4 miles   **5069** steps   ▮▮▮▮ difficulty   ◈ 45.444, -122.641

Willamette

River

Elk
Rock
Island

Spring Park
Natural Area

SE 18th Ave

SE 19th Ave

Dogwood
Park

Kellogg Creek Trail

SE Lark St

SE 20th Ave

SE Wren St

SE Bobwhite St

SE 20th

SE Bluebird St

Ave

SE Eagle St

SE Sparrow St

SE 21st Ave

Trolley
Trail

SE 22nd Ave

ction Co Rr

River Rd

SE Birk St

SE Wren St

SE McLoughlin Blvd

Kellogg Lake

99E

SE Lark St

SE 26th Ave

SE Lake Rd

SE Willard St

SE 25th Ave

P

SE 28th Ave

SE 28th Ave

SE

Kellogg
Lake Ope
Space

MILWAUKIE: DOWNTOWN AND RIVERFRONT

N

0   0

⅛   660

¼ miles

1320 feet

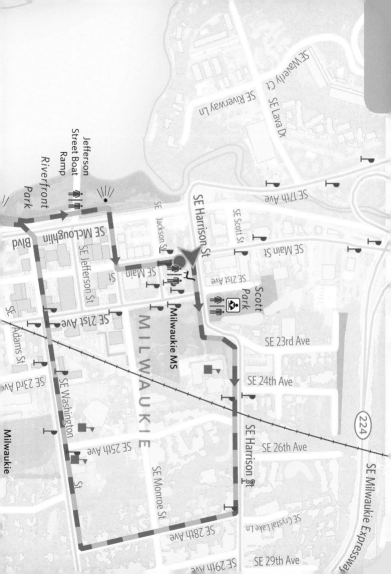

Elk Rock Island

Elk Rock Island in the Willamette River is part of a volcano that erupted 40 million years ago. Comprised of Waverly Heights Basalt, formed by lava flows, it is some of the oldest exposed rock in the Portland area. In 1910, Peter Kerr bought the island from the Rock Island Club, which had operated a dance hall there. In 1940, he gave the island to the City of Portland with the requirement that it be preserved in its natural state. The island is accessible on foot from late spring through autumn. Kerr's estate in Dunthorpe lies directly across the river. Now called the Bishop's Close, its magnificent clifftop gardens are open to the public during daylight hours.

● ● ●

Elk Rock Island with the land bridge in the foreground

Portland
Ardenwald and Johnson Creek

This walk straddles the boundary between Portland and Milwaukie and takes you along the Springwater Corridor Trail past wildlife viewing platforms at the 6-acre Tideman-Johnson Natural Area. Located in a gorge of Johnson Creek, the natural area is a favorite of local birdwatchers. Return through Milwaukie's charming Ardenwald neighborhood.

Begin at SE 45th Avenue and Crystal Springs Boulevard. Walk south on 45th and turn right on Harney. Follow Harney/45th Place to the Springwater Trail trailhead. Turn right onto the trail and walk west. Take a left into Tideman-Johnson Natural Area, walking along a paved path and elevated wooden platforms along the creek. Continue west and follow the trail that reconnects with the Springwater Trail.

At the intersection of Sherrett Street, you are standing on the Multnomah and Clackamas county boundary as well as the line between Portland and Milwaukie. Here, leave the Springwater Trail and walk east on Sherrett to 32nd; then turn right. Walk two blocks on 32nd to Roswell and turn left. Walk east, passing Ardenwald Park and Ardenwald School. At 42nd, turn left. Walk one block to Johnson Creek Boulevard. Cross it, turn right and walk back to the trailhead. Follow 45th/Harney back to the start.

2.5 miles · 5280 steps · ▮▮▮▮ difficulty · ◈ 45.465, -122.615

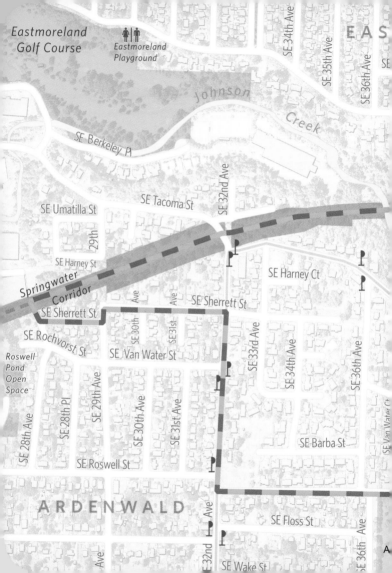

Eastmoreland
Golf Course

Eastmoreland
Playground

E A S

SE 34th Ave

SE 35th Ave

SE 36th Ave

SE

Johnson

Creek

SE Berkeley Pl

SE Umatilla St

SE Tacoma St

SE 32nd Ave

29th

SE Harney St

SE Harney Ct

Springwater

Corridor

SE Sherrett St

SE Sherrett St

Ave

Ave

SE 30th

SE 31st

SE Rochvorst St

SE Van Water St

SE 33rd Ave

SE 34th Ave

SE 36th Ave

Roswell
Pond
Open
Space

SE 28th Ave

SE 28th Pl

SE 29th Ave

SE 30th Ave

SE 31st Ave

SE Barba St

SE Van Water Ct

SE Roswell St

A R D E N W A L D

32nd

SE Floss St

SE 36th Ave

Ave

32nd

SE Wake St

A

ORELAND

SE Lexington St

PORTLAND: ARDENWALD AND JOHNSON CREEK

N

0	1/8	1/4 miles
0	660	1320 feet

SE 45th Ave

SE Crystal Springs Blvd

SE Tenino Dr

SE 37th Ave

39th

SE 41st Ave

SE Tenino St

SE 44th Ave

Errol Heights Park

St

SE

Tideman-Johnson Natural Area

SE Harney St

West Lents Floodplain

SE 45th Pl

SE Johnson Creek Blvd

Springwater Corridor

Johnson Creek Blvd

SE Brookside Dr

Van Water St

SE 40th Ave

SE 41st Ave

Ave

43rd

SE Roswell St

Roswell St

SE 42nd Ave

SE Meadowcrest Ct

SE 39th Ave

Tideman-Johnson Natural Area

The Tideman-Johnson Natural Area is named for a pioneer family whose land claim included this wilderness. The Johnson family encouraged public use of its property for recreational purposes and in 1940 donated the land to the City of Portland. Over the years, heavy use and non-native plants had degraded the land.

Recent work has reconstructed the original creek bed, created new riparian habitat, restored the natural floodplain and reestablished native plants. The natural area is home to coyotes, beavers, dozens of varieties of birds and waterfowl (including the occasional bald eagle) and is the site of a comprehensive plan to recover salmon and steelhead runs.

Milwaukie's Ardenwald Park was built on land also donated by the Johnson family. The park is a center of a close-knit community; during summer sunset concerts, children play while their parents enjoy jazz, marimba, blues and even polka music.

● ● ●

Mallard duck

Portland
Brooklyn and Rail Yards

On this 3.2-mile walk through historic Brooklyn are sites from this neighborhood's close ties to industry, from small workers' cottages to the Brooklyn rail yards where trains have run since 1868, to Bullseye Glass, a manufacturer of art and architectural glass. The walk traverses one of the city's most unique pedestrian bridges, a wooden and steel structure that carries you above trains and tracks.

Begin at SE 7th Avenue and Franklin Street; walk east on Franklin to 10th; turn right. Walk past Brooklyn Park to Rhine and turn right; on Rhine, walk to 9th, turn left and walk south to Bush. Turn left on Bush, walk two blocks and turn right on 11th, past the 1901 Sacred Heart Church. From 11th and Center, walk two blocks west on Center to a Portland Heritage Tree, a Gravenstein apple at 9th and Center. From here, walk south on 9th to Boise; turn left and walk four blocks east; at Milwaukie, jog south, cross carefully and continue east on Boise, passing the 1893 convent (now apartments) for Sacred Heart's nuns.

From Boise turn right on 16th and walk south to Holgate. Walk east on this busy road over the Brooklyn Yard, built in a filled-in slough.

East of the yard, look for a staircase to the left, at 24th. Take it to streets shared by old homes and industry. Walk north on 24th to Gladstone; turn left and then right on 22nd. Walk north to Bush. Ahead is Bullseye Glass. Go left on Bush and right on 21st, passing Bullseye's retail store. Turn left on Lafayette and walk to a wooden

(continued on page 118)

3.2 miles : 6758 steps : difficulty : 45.499, -122.658

SE Kelly St

SE 7th

SE McLoughlin Blvd

SE Franklin St

SE 8th Ave

SE 10th Ave

SE 11th Ave

12th Ave

SE

SE

Franklin

SE Pershing

SE 13th

St

Brooklyn Park

SE Haig St

Riverside Park

RhineSt

SE

SE 9th Ave

SE 11th Ave

SE

Rhine St

SE 14th Ave

Willamette

SE Rhone St

SE Rhone

St

SE 8th Ave

SE Bush St

River

SE Bush St

BROOKLYN

Springwater on the Willamette Trail

SE Center St

Broo
Sc

SE 9th Ave

Ave

SE 11th Ave

SE Boise St

SE McLoughlin

SE 10th

SE Boise

Ave

SE Cora St

SE 12th

SE 8th

SE Mall St

SE 15th Ave

Reynolds St

Holgate
Slough

pedestrian bridge. Stairs on either end of the bridge are steep and uneven; use caution. Once across, continue on Lafayette to 16th and turn right. At Pershing, turn left. Note the small cottages, once home to workers who walked to their jobs tending steam engines at the adjacent rail yards.

From Pershing, go left on 15th and right on Haig. Follow it to Milwaukie. Cross it at Pershing and take a walkway adjacent to the north side of Brooklyn Park to 11th. Turn right on 11th and left on Franklin to return to the start.

● ● ●

The rail yards

Portland
Southeast Creeks and Bridges

On this walk, ponder life at the convergence of two free-flowing streams and traverse three bridges on the Springwater Corridor Trail. After passing by the historic and peaceful Garthwick neighborhood, top off the walk at one of many great shopping and eating places in Sellwood and Westmoreland.

Begin at SE 17th Avenue and Bybee Boulevard. Walk east on Bybee to Westmoreland Park. Turn right at a path paralleling 22nd, walking along Crystal Springs Creek. Exit the park by turning right onto Lambert. Walk one block and turn left on 21st, keeping south as 21st becomes a sidewalk south of Spokane. Cross Tacoma and continue on 21st along the creek.

At Sherrett, enter Johnson Creek Park, where Crystal Springs Creek flows into Johnson Creek. Exit the park by turning right onto Marion Street. Walk one block and turn left on 19th. Walk to Ochoco to the Springwater Corridor Trail. Turn left onto the trail and cross three pedestrian/bicycle bridges over Johnson Creek, McLoughlin Boulevard and the Southern and Union Pacific train tracks.

After the third bridge, retrace your steps to Ochoco Street; walk west on Ochoco to 17th; bear left onto Andover Place and walk west to 13th. Turn right on 13th and left on Linn. Turn left on 11th, right on Ochoco, right on 9th, right on Tenino, left on 13th, right on Malden. Turn left on 16th and right on Bybee to return to the start.

4.6 miles : **9715** steps : **IIIII** difficulty

45.499, -122.658

PORTLAND: SOUTHEAST CREEKS AND BRIDGES

N

0 — ⅛ — ¼ miles

0 — 660 — 1320 feet

Oaks Amusement Park

Oaks Bottom Wildlife Refuge

SE Sellwood Blvd

Springwater on the Willamette Trail

Sellwood Park

Sellwood Riverfront Park

SE Oaks Park Way

Oaks Pioneer Church & Park

Sellwood Park Pool

Sellwood Bridge

SE Spokane St

Willamette River

SE Grand Ave

SE 6th Ave

SE 7th Ave

SE 8th Ave

SE 9th Ave

SE 11th Ave

SE 13th Ave

SE 15th Ave

SE 16th Ave

SE 14th Ave

SE Bybee Blvd

SE Rural St

SE Ogden St

SE Knapp St

Flavel St

SE Rex St

SE Malden St

SE Lambert St

SE Bidwell St

SELLWOOD

MORELAND

SE Lexington St

SE Miller St

SE Nehalem St

SE Tacoma St

SE Tenino St

SE Umatilla St

SE Harney St

SE Clatsop St

Sellwood MS

SE Sherrett St

SE Spoka

SE Marion St

SE 9th Ave

SE 11th Ave

SE 12th Ave

SE Linn St

SE 15th Pl

SE 16th Pl

SE Webber St

SE Ochoco St

Springwater Corridor

SE Exeter St

SE Andover Pl

Waverly Country Club

GARTHWICK

Milwaukie Ave

The 40-Mile Loop

In 2006, three bridges opened on the Springwater Corridor Trail, closing a large gap in the trail and reconnecting the community of Sellwood with the town of Milwaukie. The bridges represent a leap forward in the century-old plan to create a system of trails to connect neighborhoods, parks and natural areas in Portland and nearby cities. Dubbed the 40-Mile Loop, the route, much of which is complete, now comprises 140 miles linking wetlands, buttes, fields and pastures with neighborhoods and parks in the metropolitan region. The last gap in the Springwater Corridor Trail is a 1-mile section running west from 19th and Ochoco to the Springwater on the Willamette Trail section that leads into the heart of Portland.

Funding to complete this final segment has been secured. Metro and the City of Portland are working on closing the gap and finishing the trail in the next several years.

●　　●　　●

Bridge over McLoughlin

Portland
Colonial Heights and Ladd's Addition

This 2.3-mile loop travels through historic inner Southeast neighborhoods with plenty of places to eat and drink along the way. Platted in 1891, the Ladd's Addition neighborhood has one of the most unusual street layouts in the nation: a diagonal pattern surrounding five rose gardens. Getting lost on its elm-lined streets is a Portland tradition.

From SE 26th Avenue and Division Street, walk north on 26th and turn left on Sherman. Turn right on 24th. This is the Colonial Heights neighborhood. Both it and Ladd's Addition are part of the larger Hosford-Abernethy neighborhood. From 24th, turn left onto Stephens, right on 21st and left on Hawthorne.

At 16th, turn left to enter Ladd's Addition. Ahead is a diamond-shaped rose garden. Stay right on 16th, then left on Maple and right to continue on 16th to Ladd's Circle, the park in the neighborhood's center. Go right around the circle to Ladd Avenue and turn right. Follow Ladd to Division.

Cross Division and jog slightly east (left) to walk south (right) on 21st, then turn left on Ivon. Walk two blocks and turn right on 23rd and left onto Clinton, where streetcar era buildings are home to hip businesses. Follow Clinton to 26th, turn left and walk two blocks to the start.

2.3 miles : **4857** steps : ▐▐▐▐ difficulty : ◈ 45.473, -122.648

SE Powell Blvd

SE Brooklyn St

SE 15th Ave

SE 16th Ave

SE 17th Ave

SE 18th Ave

th Ave

th Ave

SE 21st Ave

SE Woodward St

SE 22nd Ave

SE 23rd Ave

SE Taggart St

SE 25th Ave

SE Clinton St

SE 26th Ave

SE 27th Ave

SE 28th Ave

SE Clinton St

SE Ivon St

SE 19th Ave

Clinton Community Garden

SE Ivon St

SE Division St

SE Tamarack Ave

SE Ladd Ave

SE Cypress Ave

Abernethy ES

SE Orange Ave

SE Hickory St

ABERNETHY—

HOSFORD—

SE Caruthers St

SE Sherman St

SE Caruthers St

SE Grant St

Hosford MS

Piccol... Park

PORTLAND: COLONIAL HEIGHTS AND LADD'S ADDITION

N

0   0

660   ⅛

1320 feet   ¼ miles

0

Inner Southeast History

Volunteers nurture the century old elms in Ladd's Addition, working to prevent Dutch Elm Disease from wiping out this city treasure.

Once-large lots in inner Southeast neighborhoods were home to Italian-American truck farmers in the early twentieth century. Through the 1950s, they sold their produce at various venues in town, including the Grand Central Market on SE Morrison, and delivered it to homes. Produce Row in the Central Eastside Industrial Area is part of this heritage.

In the 1960s, streets south of Division were slated for demolition for the Mount Hood Freeway; its alignment would have followed Ivon Street along the route of this walk, severing the neighborhood and turning Division into a frontage road. ODOT began buying properties for demolition, but by 1974, opposition stopped the freeway.

Rhododendrons at Ladd's Circle

Portland
Sellwood and Oaks Bottom

This walk combines the best of the city's urban landscape with its natural areas. On it, stroll the Sellwood neighborhood's scenic blufftop streets and travel the multiuse Springwater Corridor Trail through Oaks Bottom, a 140-acre birdwatcher's paradise along the Willamette River. Bring binoculars.

Begin at the Sellwood Library, SE 13th Avenue and Bidwell Street. Walk south on 13th and turn right onto Spokane. Follow Spokane downhill; after the railroad tracks, turn right onto the Springwater Trail. On the left is Sellwood Riverfront Park and then Oaks Amusement Park. On the right is the Oaks Bottom Wildlife Refuge. Across from Oaks Park, pass over a pedestrian tunnel that leads into the refuge. Continue on the Springwater Trail to a pedestrian tunnel under the railroad tracks. Turn right into the tunnel to enter Oaks Bottom. Follow the paved path through the refuge uphill to a parking lot at Mitchell Street and Milwaukie Avenue.

From the lot, turn right on Milwaukie, then right on Ellis, left on 15th, right on Henry and left on 14th. From 14th, turn right on Bybee. Along the bluff top, Bybee turns into 13th. From 13th, turn right on Knapp and then walk along Sellwood Boulevard with its spectacular views of downtown and Oaks Bottom. A heritage white oak grows at 1224. Turn left on 11th, left on Lambert and then right on 13th to return to the start.

3.8 miles : **8025** steps : ▮▮▮ difficulty : ◆ 45.467, -122.653

Willamette

Sellwood Bridge

Sellwood River front Park

Springwater Trail

SE Oaks Park Way

Oaks Amusement Park

SE Grand Ave

Sellwood Park

SE 6th Ave

Sellwood Park Pool

SE 7th Ave

SE 8th Ave

SE Tacoma St

SE 9th Ave

SE Nehalem St

SE 11th Ave

SE Lambert St

SE Sellwood Blvd

Pond

SE Umatilla St

SE Spokane St

SE Bidwell St

SE Malden St

SE Rex St

SE Flavel St

SE 13th Ave

Sellwood Community Center

SE 15th Ave

SE Lexington St

SE Knapp St

SE Ogden St

SE Rural St

SE Bybee Blvd

M O R E L A N D

S E L L W O O D

SE 16th Ave

SE Milwaukie Ave

SE Terino St

SE 17th Ave

SE 17th Ave

SE Nehalem St

SE Bidwell St

SE 18th Ave

SE 19th Ave

N

0   0
¼   1320
½ miles   2640 feet

River

Toe Island

Ross Island

Holgate Slough

Oaks Bottom Wildlife Refuge

Springwater on the Willamette Trail

SE Henry St
SE 13th Ave
SE Carlton St
SE Martins St
SE Yukon St
SE Ramona St
SE Milwaukie Ave
SE Knight St
SE Reedway St
SE Ellis St
SE Harold St
SE Insley St
SE Mitchell St
SE McLoughlin Blvd

th Ave
SE Duke St
SE Tolman St
SE Henry St
SE 17th Ave
SE 20th Ave
SE Tolman St
SE Yukon St
SE Knight St
SE Reedway St
SE Harold St
SE 17th Ave
SE 18th Ave
SE 19th Ave
SF Claybourne St

P

A Home for Wildlife in the City

Oaks Bottom is a floodplain wetland of the Willamette River. Part of it had become a landfill, a common fate of wetlands in urban areas. Filled areas exist at the north end of the bottomland where fill was placed from the I-405 freeway construction, and at the south end, which was a former garbage dump. In 1969, the landfill's owner intended to develop the area as an industrial park. The city purchased the land and planned a developed park; by the 1980s, however, growing interest in preserving urban natural areas led to the abandonment of those plans. In 1988, Oaks Bottom became the city's first wildlife refuge. Watch for great blue herons, which thrive here in close proximity to their rookeries on nearby Ross Island. Over 100 species of birds have been sighted here.

● ● ●

Great blue heron

Portland
Westmoreland to Crystal Springs

Discover Crystal Springs Rhododendron Garden, blazing with color April through June with more than 2,500 rhododendrons, azaleas and companion plants. Spring-fed Crystal Springs Lake attracts many species of birds. The springs emerge from Reed Canyon, hidden in Reed College.

Begin this 2.0-mile (one-way) walk at SE 17th Avenue and Bybee Boulevard, near the heart of Westmoreland. Walk east on the north side of Bybee; across the railroad tracks is the Eastmoreland neighborhood. Follow Bybee as it curves north and becomes 28th Avenue.

Just north of Woodstock Boulevard, turn left into the Crystal Springs Rhododendron Garden. Begun in 1950 as a test garden by the Portland Chapter of the American Rhododendron Society, the garden found a home here after a potential site on SW Terwilliger Boulevard was deemed too steep. This once scrubby and weed-choked island and peninsula was cleared, and landscape architects designed today's inviting and serene layout. A fee is charged some days. See www.portlandonline.com for more information.

Leave the garden by crossing 28th and then turning left. Turn right on Botsford Drive, into the Reed College campus. Walk east and connect to a series of trails around Reed Canyon's creek, lake and springs.

Wander through the beautiful Reed campus or retrace your steps to the start where you'll find many places to shop and eat along Bybee and Milwaukie.

4.0 miles : **8448** steps : difficulty : 45.473, -122.648

SE Ellis St

SE Reedway St

SE McLoughlin Blvd

SE 26th Ave

SE Reedway St

SE 17th Ave

SE 19th Ave

0th Ave

SE 21st Ave

P

Eastmorelar

Golf

Course

SE

PORTLAND: WESTMORELAND TO CRYSTAL SPRINGS

N

0   ⅛   ¼ miles

0   660   1320 feet

SE Yukon St

99E

SE Tolman St

SELLWOOD-

MORELAND

SE Claybourne St

SE 23rd Ave

SE 22nd Ave

SE 21st Ave

SE 19th Ave

SE 17th Ave

SE McLoughlin Blvd

Glenwood St

0th Ave

SE Bybee

Westmoreland
Park

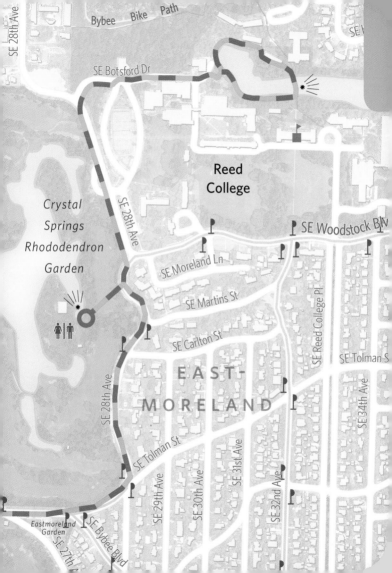

Reed College Campus

Reed College is one of the city's most beautiful places, with brick manor-like buildings, manicured grounds and a deep tree canopy. Visit www.reed.edu/trees for photographs and descriptions of 100 species of trees on campus along with detailed maps on where to find them.

Another sort of beauty lies hidden on the campus: 26 acres of wildlife habitat nestled in a spring-fed canyon. In the early 1900s, when this land was the Crystal Springs Farm, a 10 foot dam on Crystal Springs Creek created Reed Lake here. One hundred years later, a fish ladder corrected this impediment to fish passage. Also around 2000, a swimming pool was removed from the canyon as efforts began to restore the land to its natural state. Reed Canyon is a treasure, from its upper reaches, where springs emerge from the hillside, to the lower end, with its lake and the restored flow of Crystal Springs Creek.

● ● ●

Old Dorm Block on the Reed College campus

Portland
Mount Tabor

Explore the paths and historical features of one of Portland's finest parks, home to beautiful reservoirs and a remnant volcanic cinder cone. This walk combines stairs, closed roadways and unimproved paths as you climb and descend the summit. Awesome views will be the payoff.

From SE 60th Avenue and Salmon Street, walk south on 60th to steps up to Reservoir 6. Take the steps which end at a walkway around the reservoir. Walk around either end of the reservoir to the other side; there, take a set of steps up to Reservoir 5. At the top is Reservoir Loop Drive. Cross it to arrive at Reservoir 5.

Continue south on Reservoir Loop Drive to a trail around Poison Oak Hill. There is no signage but this trail begins just past the stone building at the south end of the reservoir. At the Y continue right. This trail runs through woods above Reservoir Loop Drive and after going around Poison Oak Hill crosses the road. Continue to the trail on the north side of Reservoir 1. This trail heads east and then north through the forest, climbing to Harvey Scott Circle, a roadway around the summit. From the statue of Harvey, head northwest to the north end of the summit.

Descend on trails past a playground to a parking lot and restrooms. From there, head west to the amphitheatre carved into the peak's cinder cone. By the amphitheatre is a basketball court. Head downhill on the trail behind it, taking the trail that veers left somewhat following Salmon Way downhill but going through a small wooded valley to Salmon Street. Continue west on Salmon to the starting point.

2.1 miles   **4435** steps   ▮▮▮▮ difficulty   ◆ 45.514, -122.602

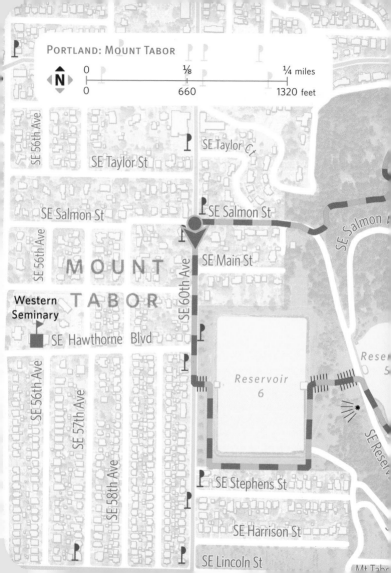

PORTLAND: MOUNT TABOR

N

| 0 | ⅛ | ¼ miles |

| 0 | 660 | 1320 feet |

SE 56th Ave

SE Taylor St

SE Taylor Ct

SE 56th Ave

SE Salmon St

SE Salmon St

SE Salmon

MOUNT

SE Main St

TABOR

SE 60th Ave

Western
Seminary

SE Hawthorne Blvd

Reservoir
6

Reser
S

SE 56th Ave

SE 57th Ave

SE 58th Ave

SE Reserv

SE Stephens St

SE Harrison St

SE Lincoln St

Mt Tabo

SE Morrison St

SE Belmont St

Yamhill Ct

SE Yamhill St

SE 71st Ave

SE 72nd Ave

SE Yamhill St

SE Park Dr

SE Taylor St

SE North Tabor Dr

SE 73rd Ave

SE Salmon St

SE 71st Ave

Mount

SE Harvey Scott Cir

SE Tabor Summit Dr

SE Main St

SE Main St

Tabor

SE Madison St

SE Hawthorne Blvd

statue

SE Clay St

Park

SE Market St

SE East Tabor Dr

SE 74th Ave

SE Stephens St

Res.
1

SE 72nd Ave

SE Harrison St

SE Harrison Dr

SE Harrison Ct

SE Harrison Ct

u Access Rd

Art in the Park

At the top of the park is a bronze statue of Harvey W. Scott, editor of the Oregonian from 1865-1872 and 1877 until his death in 1910. A gift of Scott's widow Margaret and family, the sculpture is the work of Gutzon Borglum. It was completed in the 1930s while Borglum was working on his sculpture of four American presidents on Mount Rushmore in South Dakota's Black Hills.

Mount Tabor's elevation and central location made this an ideal place for the city to store water piped from the Bull Run Reservoir east of the Sandy River. The open-air reservoirs, now a long-outdated means of storing water, were built between 1894 and 1911 along with reservoirs on the west side of town, in Washington Park. The reservoirs and their gatehouses, which incorporate hand-cut stonework and wrought iron, were placed on the National Register of Historic Places in 2004.

Open-air reservoir at Mount Tabor Park

South Region

	D	N	P	C	H	L
A. Lake Oswego: Millennium Plaza and beyond *p. 141*	4.4	•		•	•	•
B. Lake Oswego: Old River Road *p. 145*	2.6	•			•	•
C. Oregon City: McLoughlin Historic District *p. 149*	1.5			•	•	•
D. West Linn: Willamette Historic District *p. 155*	1.6			•	•	•
E. Wilsonville: Memorial Park and Murase ... *p. 159*	3.4	•		•		
F. Sherwood: Old Town *p. 163*	1.0	•		•	•	•
G. Tigard and Tualatin: Fanno Creek Greenway *p. 167*	2.8	•				•

D   Distance in Miles   C   City Cruise
N   Nature Walk   H   History Walk
P   Power Walk   L   Lunchtime Stroll

Lake Oswego
Millennium Plaza and beyond

Beautiful Lake Oswego has reclaimed its industrial waterfront, turning it into a series of riverside parks. This 2.2-mile (one-way) walk takes you from the gleaming Millennium Plaza Park with its views of Lakewood Bay and adjoining shops and restaurants, back to the origin of the once gritty mining town of Oswego.

Begin at 200 First Street at Millennium Plaza Park, head east to State Street and turn right. Cross State Street at Foothills Road and walk north, then east on Foothills adjacent to the station for the Willamette Shore Trolley, which runs between Portland and Lake Oswego. Past a parking lot on the left, take the Kincaid Curlicue Corridor trail. It leads to Foothills Park along the Willamette River. Follow this trail to Roehr Park and turn right (south), continuing to the Water Sports Center, a recreation facility owned by the city and operated by Lake Oswego Community Rowing.

From the Water Sports Center, walk back to State Street via Oswego Pointe Drive, turning south (left) on State. At Leonard, turn left into Old Town. Beyond the intersection of Leonard and Durham is a giant fir, the Peg Tree. Early settlers hung a lantern on a peg in its trunk to light town meetings held under its branches. From Leonard, turn right at Furnace Street, which leads into the riverside George Rogers Park, site of the only remaining nineteenth century iron furnace on the West Coast.

Return to Millennium Plaza Park by walking northward through Old Town and then north on State Street.

4.4 miles : 9293 steps : ▮▮▮▮ difficulty : ◈ 45.418, -122.664

N

0

0

660

1/8

1320 feet

1/4 miles

Dyer St

Ash St

Maple St

Oak St

Yates St

O S W E G O

Lund St

Ash St

ullock St

Gens

Pacific Hwy

43

Headlee Ln

Old River R

Willamette Greenway Trail

Ellen Bergis Nature Reserve

Mcvey Ave

Pacific Hwy

Oswego Creek

S O U T H   L A K E

Fairmont Rd

Lakewood Ave

Lake Oswego Swim Park

Middle Crest Rd

S Sta

George Rogers Park

Green St

Ladd St

Wilbur St

Durha

Furr

River to River Trail

Willamett

SE River Forest Dr

Oswego Lake

Lake Bay Ct

Oswego

LAKE OSWEGO

4th St

B Ave

3rd St

Evergreen Rd

2nd St

Millennium Plaza Park

North Shore Rd

1st St

N State St

A Ave

43

Leonard St

Village Ln

Oswego Pointe Dr

Foothills Rd

Trolley Depot

Oswego Pointe Dr

Foothills Rd

Oswego Pointe Dr

Foothills Dr

Pointe Dr.

Foothills Rd

Foothills Park

Water Sports Center

Roehr Park/ Amphitheater

River

A Fiery Past

Albert Durham named Oswego in 1847 after his New York birthplace; he founded a sawmill on Sucker Creek (now Oswego Creek). At George Rogers Park on Oswego Creek is the town's first blast furnace, from 1867, where ore from nearby Iron Mountain was refined.

Foothills Park is located on riverside land that was home in the 1880s to a pipe foundry and a blast furnace that had succeeded the first furnace on Sucker Creek. Cast iron pipe constructed here still carries water from the Bull Run watershed into Portland and nearby cities. The last industrial use was a woodchip processing facility, which closed in the late 1990s. In 2002, the City of Lake Oswego bought the land for a park and construction began in 2005.

In 1960, Oswego merged with Lake Grove; the combined towns were renamed "Lake Oswego."

Foothills Park

Lake Oswego
Old River Road

This paved 1.3-mile path along the historic river road that once connected Oswego to Willamette Falls travels scenically along the Willamette River, starting at George Rogers Park. Highlights include a waterfall, river views, deep foliage and the company of other like-minded walkers and runners.

Begin at the corner of Green and Furnace streets at George Rogers Park. Walk south, crossing a bridge over Oswego Creek. Once over the creek, take the paved trail to the left. This is the Old River Road Willamette Greenway Trail. Watch for the seasonal waterfall on the right. At the intersection of Glenmorrie/Old River Road, notice the large concrete structure in the river. It was a log hoist built in 1905 by Crown Willamette Paper Company and operated until the 1920s. The house opposite the hoist, on the right side of the path, was built by the company to house the manager of the log hoist and the company's tug boat operation. The house sits on the edge of South Town, one of Lake Oswego's earliest neighborhoods.

At Old River Road, the carless section of trail ends. Turn around here and retrace your steps or continue along the trail as it follows Old River Road (the automobile portion). At the city limits of West Linn, the path stops.

2.6 miles : **5491** steps : difficulty : 45.410, -122.660

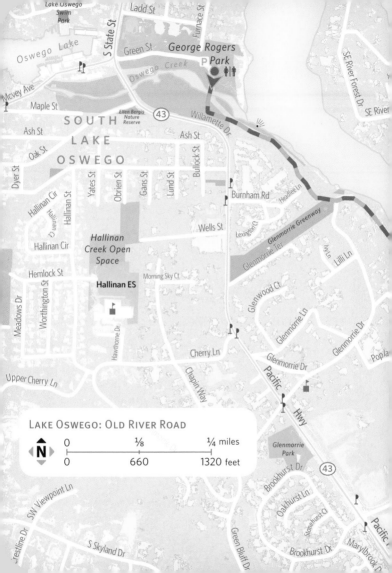

Lake Oswego Swim Park

Oswego Lake

Ladd St

Furnace St

Green St

George Rogers Park

P

Oswego Creek

SE River Forest Dr

S State St

Mcvey Ave

Maple St

Ellen Bergis Nature Reserve

SOUTH

Ash St

LAKE

Oak St

OSWEGO

Ash St

Willamette Dr

(43)

SE River

Dyer St

Yates St

Obrien St

Gans St

Lund St

Bullock St

Hallinan Cir

Hallinan St

Hallinan Ct

Burnham Rd

Headlee Ln

Hallinan Cir

Wells St

Lexington Ct

Glenmorrie Greenway

Glenmorrie Ter

Hemlock St

Hallinan Creek Open Space

Morning Sky Ct

Glenwood Ct

Glenmorrie Ter

Ivy Ln

Lilli Ln

Meadows Dr

Worthington St

Hallinan ES

Hawthorne Dr

Glenwood Ln

Glenmorrie Ln

Glenmorrie Dr

Cherry Ln

Chapin Way

Glenmorrie Dr

Pacific Hwy

Popla

Upper Cherry Ln

Lake Oswego: Old River Road

◀**N**▶

0	⅛	¼ miles
0	660	1320 feet

Glenmorrie Park

(43)

Crestline Dr

SW Viewpoint Ln

Brookhurst Dr

Oakhurst Ln

Stonehurst Ct

Pacific

S Skyland Dr

Green Bluff Dr

Brookhurst Dr

Marylbrook

George Rogers Park

George Rogers Park is located in the Old Town area of Lake Oswego at Oswego Creek's confluence with the Willamette River. The site was inhabited by Native Americans and much used by early settlers for its water power and river landing. It was also the home of the city's industrial roots, as the location of Oswego's first blast furnace. It began operating in 1867, refining the iron ore found in the hills north of Oswego Lake (then called Sucker Lake). The blast furnace's chimney stack remains and park features mimic its elegant arched form. Other vestiges are less obvious, but the recently renovated park's great river views, beach, trails and picnic areas make it a destination to explore. The iron industry left Oswego in 1894, a victim of cheaper iron mined in the East. By the 1910s, the town began its transition to the thriving community Lake Oswego is today.

● ● ●

George Rogers Park

Oregon City McLoughlin Historic District

1.5 miles · 3168 steps · ▮▮▮▮▮ difficulty · ◈ 45.355, -122.604

OREGON CITY: MCLOUGHLIN HISTORIC DISTRICT

In this 1.5-mile Oregon City walk, you'll ride one of the nation's only municipal elevators, stroll a blufftop promenade overlooking thundering Willamette Falls and pass some of the state's oldest homes, including the 1846 John McLoughlin House, final home of the "Father of Oregon." Several of the homes passed are open as museums.

Begin at 606 John Adams Street at the Carnegie Center, built in 1913 as the Oregon City Library. It sits on a block donated to the city by McLoughlin in 1850. From the center's front steps, walk across John Adams for a look at the 1923 Fire Station and City Hall, at 7th Street, before walking south on John Adams to the oldest home in Oregon, the 1845 Francis Ermatinger House, at 619 6th Street. In 1845, a coin flip inside determined Portland's name. The home sat originally on the lower level of Oregon City, next to the river.

Turn right on 6th and pass the Stevens-Crawford House, a 1908 Foursquare, now a museum, full of the ephemera and furnishings of early to mid twentieth century life. Continue on 6th, turn left at Center and right at 5th, following it to the McLoughlin Promenade. From here enjoy views of Willamette Falls and the industries that since the 1840s have harnessed its power. The promenade's rockwork was constructed in the 1930s as a work relief project. Turn right onto the promenade and pass the 1882 Queen Anne home of C.D. Latourette,

Carnegie Center

Oregon City in the nineteenth century

at 503 High St.; and the home of M. D. Latourette, a Foursquare from 1914, at 509. The Latourettes are one of the city's most prominent families.

Follow the promenade to the Oregon City Municipal Elevator; it connects the town's river and bluff levels. Rides are free. (If you want, add about 0.25 mile and a stair climb by taking the elevator down, then turning right and ascending a beautiful staircase that climbs the hill next to a stream and ends at the McLoughlin House.) From the elevator, walk north on the walkway, cross High Street, walk east (uphill) on 7th and turn left at Center to pass the McLoughlin House. It also was originally located on the lower level but moved to this site in 1909.

From Center turn right on 8th. At 812 John Adams is the 1930 Elizabeth Clark house, the first in the county to have colored plumbing fixtures. Then turn left onto Jefferson to see the Morris Holman Residence (810 Jefferson), a one-of-a-kind English cottage. From Jefferson, turn right on 10th and right on Madison. At 910 is the Dr. Ross and Ruth Latourette Eaton Residence from 1928. He was a physician; she was an osteopath. Continue on Madison to 4th and turn right and right again on Jefferson. At 415 Jefferson is an 1874 home built by F. O. McCown, who co-founded the Oregon City Electric Company and also worked to improve the Barlow Road. At Jefferson and 5th (715 5th) is the 1895 Judge Thomas Ryan House, with the city's only intact carriage house.

Turn left at 6th and walk one block to John Adams. At the corner is the Atkinson Memorial Church, with windows by Portland's famed Povey Brothers. Across the street is the Carnegie Center.

Willamette River

99E

McLoughlin Blvd

DOWNTOWN

8th St

9th

Main St

7th St

6th St

Singer

McLou
Hous

Oregon City
Municipal
Elevator

5th St

Railroad Ave

McLoughlin Promenade

6th

High

MCLOUGHL

St

99E

5th St

McLoughlin Blvd

4th St

Center St

High

St

John Ad

3rd St

Washington

3rd

OREGON CITY: MCLOUGHLIN HISTORIC DISTRICT

N

0	¹⁄₁₆	⅛ miles
0	330	660 feet

Oregon's First City

In 1829 John McLoughlin, who was then head of the Hudson's Bay Company's Fort Vancouver, claimed land at Willamette Falls for England. It was a time when ownership of the Oregon Territory (an area that included parts of British Columbia south to today's Oregon and east to parts of Montana and Wyoming) was in dispute. With American settlers moving into the region, English claims were increasingly tenuous. In 1842, McLoughlin named the site at Willamette Falls "Oregon City" and platted it for England. But by 1845, settlers from the United States voted the town the seat of the Oregon Territory's first provisional government. McLoughlin retired from his work and joined the settlers, building his home here in 1845. In 1846, the international boundary between English Canada and the United States was set at its current location.

Willamette Falls

West Linn
Willamette Historic District

West Linn's Willamette Historic District began as a company town established in 1893 by Willamette Falls Electric. In 1913, a typhoid epidemic led Willamette to annex to West Linn to obtain a better water source. The walk takes you through Willamette's historic streets, with a stop at Willamette Park, located at the confluence of the Tualatin and Willamette rivers. Here you can picnic along the river while watching herons and sandpipers eat their lunch.

From 12th Street and Willamette Falls Drive, turn south on 12th and then right onto 6th Avenue. From 6th, turn left on 14th Street, and walk one block to 5th Avenue. At 1847 is an 1897 Queen Anne owned by Nicholas Walden, an early developer of Willamette. Ahead is Willamette School, from 1949. An earlier school, built in 1896, was enclosed by wooden fences to protect kids at recess from roaming cattle.

From 5th, turn right on 12th. At 1724 4th, note the cow prints in the sidewalk along the home's 14th Avenue side. From 4th, turn left on 14th Street and follow it to Tualatin Avenue. Turn right to walk on the bridge for views of the Tualatin River. For most of its 83-mile run, the river is slow and meandering. Here, it steps up the pace and rushes over a rocky bottom just before joining the Willamette.

(continued on page 158)

1.6 miles ⋮ **3376** steps ⋮ ▮▮▮ difficulty ⋮ ◈ 45.344, -122.653

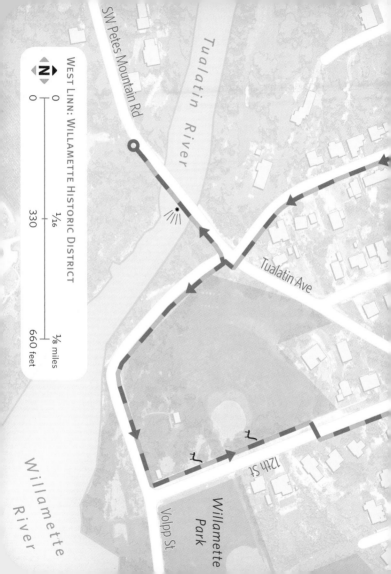

SW Petes Mountain Rd

Tualatin River

WEST LINN: WILLAMETTE HISTORIC DISTRICT

N

| 0 | 1/16 | 1/8 miles |
| 0 | 330 | 660 feet |

Tualatin Ave

Willamette River

Willamette Park

Volpp St

12th St

Willamette Falls Dr.

8th Ave

13th St

14th St

5th Ave

Knapps Alley

6th Ave

13th St

4th Ave

12th St

Willamette Primary School

W I L L A M E T T E

H I S T O R I C

D I S T R I C T

5th Ave

11th St

10th St

lies Way

Come off the bridge and turn right into Willamette Park, where sediments carried from the Tualatin's 712 square mile watershed have created a nice beach.

Exit Willamette Park on 12th, the main park road. Turn left on 4th and right on 13th to see more historic district homes. At Willamette Falls Drive turn right to return to the start.

Plan your walk for a Wednesday to visit the West Linn Farmers and Artists Market at the corner of 13th Street and Willamette Falls Drive. The market runs from mid-May to mid-September, from 4:30 to 8:30 p.m. and features local produce, art, music and food. When the market is not in session, this area offers plenty of restaurants, coffee houses and shops to enjoy at the end of the walk.

Downtown West Linn

Wilsonville
Memorial Park and Murase Plaza

126-acre Memorial Park encompasses the best of Oregon, with its people-centered Murase Plaza, community garden on Kolbe Lane, forested natural areas adjacent to Boeckman Creek and 0.5 mile of Willamette River frontage.

Begin at Murase Plaza, Wilsonville Road and Memorial Drive. This upper portion of Memorial Park transitions between developed, more urban areas near Wilsonville Road and the wooded, natural character of the lower park. From the plaza, head south on the trail past the child's play area and historic barn. As you descend the trail, Boeckman Creek is to the east. Fish barriers have been removed from the creek and its banks restored with native vegetation. After passing the lower barn, join the Central Loop Trail by turning left toward the off-leash dog area. Here, access undeveloped park areas: open meadows and primitive trails along the Willamette River and Boeckman Creek. Continue on the Central Loop Trail past two picnic shelters and around the athletic fields or walk through the wooded area along the Willamette to the public boat dock.

Other park facilities include a skatepark, basketball courts, tennis courts, playgrounds and a sand volleyball court. Memorial Park is also home to a community garden, east of Murase Plaza along Kolbe Lane. For a longer walk, take any of the trails off the Central Loop Trail into less developed natural areas. Many trails have level grades and are ADA accessible.

3.4 miles : **7172** steps : ▮▮▮▮ difficulty : ◆ 45.301, -122.758

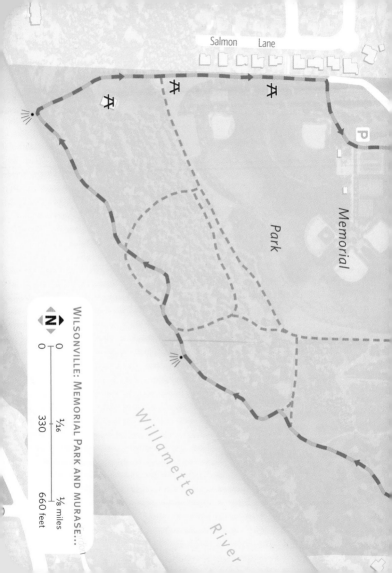

Salmon Lane

Park

Memorial

P

Willamette River

WILSONVILLE: MEMORIAL PARK AND MURASE...

N

0   1/16   1/8 miles
0   330   660 feet

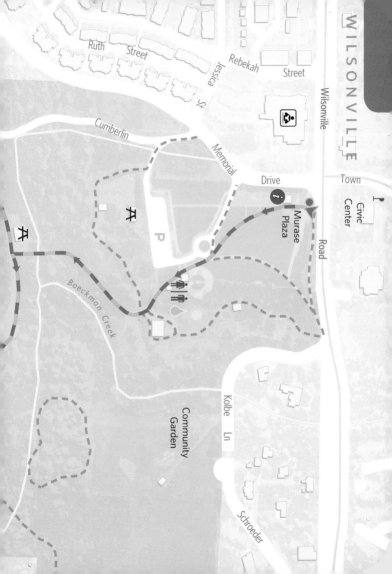

Murase Plaza

In 2006, Wilsonville unveiled the 22-acre Murase Plaza, named to honor Robert Murase (muir-ah-zee), a landscape architect whose vision was to create connections among citizens through natural and architectural beauty. Murase Plaza mixes water play, play structures and formal plantings with apple and walnut orchards from the land's days as a farm. Murase also designed Beaverton's Nike World Headquarters and the Japanese American Historical Plaza at Portland's Waterfront Park.

Along the Central Loop Trail, goats have been working since 2002 to eradicate non-native English ivy. Each summer, the public can participate in a goat day event, to learn about the role goats play in controlling invasive plant species.

● ● ●

Fountain at Murase Plaza

Sherwood
Old Town

Sherwood was platted out in 1889 around the rail depot. This walk explores Old Town Sherwood's historic buildings and loops through the woods and wetlands of Stella Olsen Memorial Park before returning to Old Town with its many shops, restaurants and antique stores.

Begin at SW Pine and 2nd streets. In the northwest corner is one of the state's largest Atlas cedars. Walk south on Pine. At the southwest corner of Pine and 1st is the site of the livery stable, origin of the great fire of 1911 that destroyed much of downtown.

From Pine, turn right onto Railroad Street. A visitor information center is at Pine and Railroad. The Old Sherwood Hotel, from the 1890s, sits at the northeast corner of Washington and Railroad. A vital element to any railroad town, the hotel also doubled as the town bank for a time. Across Railroad is the Graves Cannery, from 1918. It processed fruits picked by child laborers from nearby farms. It closed in 1971.

Where Washington crosses Railroad is the site of a civic protest. In the 1910s, homes had been built on the south side of Railroad. Residents needed to safely cross the tracks, but the Southern Pacific refused a request for a signaled crossing. Citizens then built a crossing during the middle of the night and spent the next 24 hours in a constant parade across it. The necessary signal was soon installed.

(continued on page 166)

1.0 miles : 2112 steps : difficulty : 45.357, -122.841

SW Lee Dr

SW Travis Ct

Sherwood HS

SW Villa Rd

Stella Olsen
Memorial Park

SW

SW

SW Sherwood Blvd

■ Sherwood MS

SW Ash St

SW Pine St

SW 2nd St

SW Oak St

SW Washington St

SW 1st St

SW Oregon St

i

S H E R W O O D

SW Main St

SW Railroad St

SW Columbia St

SW Pine St

Veterans
Memorial
Park

P

SW Washington

SW Main St

SW Columbia St

SW Willamette St

SHERWOOD: OLD TOWN

N

| 0 | | 1/16 | | 1/8 miles |

| 0 | | 330 | | 660 feet |

On the left between Washington and Main is the site of the town's train depot. After Park Street, the road jogs right and becomes SW Villa Road. Take Villa into Stella Olsen Memorial Park, centered on two islands created by the meandering Cedar Creek as it flows north to the Tualatin River. Turn right to walk along a boardwalk over wetlands. At the end, cross the creek. A covered picnic area is to the left. Continue through the park to the sidewalk on Washington Street.

Turn right on Washington past historic homes. At 2nd is the charming 150-square-foot Rudy Olsen Gas Pump Park. Turn left on 1st. At the corner is the 1911 Colfelt building, where a saloon has operated since 1896. At Pine, turn left and walk one block to the start.

• • •

Rudy Olsen Gas Pump Park

Tigard and Tualatin
Fanno Creek Greenway Trail

This 1.4-mile (one-way) walk along the Fanno Creek Greenway Trail traverses three towns and 200 acres of greenspace including Tigard's Cook Park, Durham's City Park and Tualatin's Tualatin Community Park, as well as land owned by Clean Water Services. Creek and river crossings, wetlands, ponds and an oak savannah are some of the highlights.

Begin at SW Durham Road and Hall Boulevard. Hall changes name to 85th Avenue south of Durham Road. Walk south on 85th Avenue 2,000 feet to the trail entrance across from the Clean Water Services office. Follow the trail through a former pasture for dairy cows to Cook Park's east parking lot. From the parking lot, continue on a concrete trail through the Tupling Butterfly Garden in Cook Park. Opened in 2004 adjacent to Tualatin River wetlands, the garden honors Kristine Ann Tupling, whose donation funded the flowering landscape, walkways and viewing gazebo here.

From the garden, follow a pathway along the Tualatin River to a railroad trestle. Pass under the trestle on a trail that leads into Durham City Park. Turn right and walk across the Ki-a-kuts Bicycle and Pedestrian Bridge over the river. Once across, follow the trail through the river floodplain into Tualatin Community Park.

Retrace your steps to the start or follow Tualatin Road south to Boones Ferry Road. Turn left and walk two blocks to the bus stop at Martinazzi Avenue.

2.8 miles : **5913** steps : ▮▮▮▯ difficulty : ◈ 45.404, -122.764

SW 92nd Ave

Cook

Butterfly
Garden

Millen Dr

SW Martha St

SW Oak

SW Durham Rd

Harford Loop

SW 88th Ave

Tigard HS

SW 87th Ave

SW Stratford St

SW Avon St

SW Avon Pl

SW 85th Ave

SW Hall Blv

SW Colton Ln

SW Durham Ln

SW Shaffer Ln

Greenway

Durham
City

Trail

Fanno Creek

one Dr

SW Durham Rd

SW Bond St

Durham
HS

SW Alder St

SW Binddale Ct

SW Findlay Dr

SW Afton Ln

SW 77th Ter

SW 76th Ave

SW Upper Boones Ferry Rd

TIGARD AND TUALATIN: FANNO CREEK GREENWAY TRAIL

N

0	1/8	1/4 miles
0	660	1320 feet

Parks on the Tualatin River

Cook Park's 79 acres along the Tualatin River offer classic park facilities: ball fields, horseshoe pits, a fishing dock and picnic shelters. Here, every June is the Tigard Festival of Balloons, three days when hot air balloons color the skies above carnival rides, a fun run, barbecue contests and a craft fair.

Connected to Cook Park is Durham City Park, centered around the last winding bends of Fanno Creek before it joins the Tualatin River.

Across the Ki-a-kuts Bicycle and Pedestrian Bridge is Tualatin Community Park, 27 acres with a boat ramp, sports fields, ball courts, a playground and skatepark. The bridge is named for Ki-a-kuts, the last chief of the Atfalati Native Americans. The Atfalati, also called the Tuality, lived throughout the Tualatin River basin, from the river's origins west of Gaston to its confluence with the Willamette River.

● ● ●

Ki-a-kuts Bicycle and Pedestrian Bridge

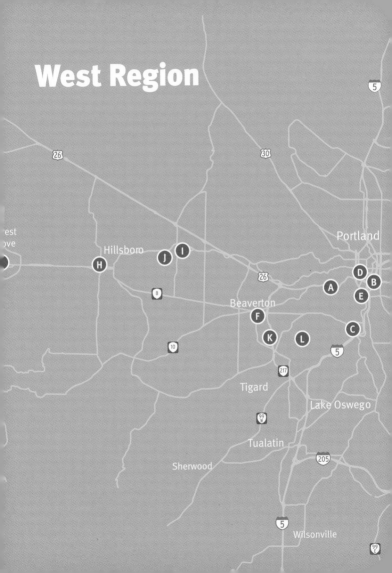

West Region

West Region

	D	N	P	C	H	L
A. Portland: 4T– Trail, Tram, Trolley and Train *p. 173*	3.95	•	•	•		
B. Portland: Willamette Waterfront *p. 177*	2.6			•	•	•
C. Portland: Hillsdale to the River *p. 181*	4.0	•	•	•	•	
D. Portland: Portland Heights to Zoo *p. 185*	5.6		•	•	•	
E. Portland: South Portland *p. 189*	4.7	•	•	•	•	
F. Beaverton: Downtown to Round *p. 195*	2.8	•		•		•
G. Forest Grove: Pacific University ... *p. 199*	2.4	•		•	•	•
H. Hillsboro: Downtown *p. 205*	2.4			•	•	•
I. Hillsboro: Rock Creek Trail *p. 209*	3.2	•				•
J. Hillsboro: Orenco and Orenco Station *p. 213*	2.2			•	•	•
K. Tigard: Fanno Creek Greenway Trail *p. 219*	5.4	•		•		
L. Beaverton: Fanno Creek Greenway Trail *p. 223*	2.3	•			•	•

D   Distance in Miles

N   Nature Walk

P   Power Walk

C   City Cruise

H   History Walk

L   Lunchtime Stroll

Portland
4T – Trail, Tram, Trolley and Train

For the ultimate Portland excursion, begin with a walk up the Marquam Trail to the city's highest point, Council Crest; pass through the campus of Oregon Health and Science University (OHSU), the city's largest employer; then ride free down the Portland Aerial Tram to the developing South Waterfront District. Head north on the streetcar (trolley) and stop at one of downtown's many attractions before returning to the start via the MAX train. The walking portion of the route, from the Zoo to the top of the tram, is 3.95 miles.

Note: The aerial tram is closed on major holidays. Visit www.portlandtram.org for dates.

Begin at the Washington Park MAX station at 4001 SW Canyon Road in Portland. Walk south along the Zoo toward the roar of the Sunset Highway. Cross over it on the elevated roadway, Knight Boulevard, walking on its left (east) side. Cross the highway ramp and turn left to walk east. Turn right at a trailhead for the Marquam Trail. Follow the trail as it climbs to Patton Road and Heather Lane.

Turn right on Patton. At the intersection of Humphrey, Patton and Talbot, go uphill onto Talbot. Follow it to an entrance to the Marquam Trail in Council Crest Park. Follow the paved path and then a sidewalk on the left that brings you to the top of Council Crest, at elevation 1,073 feet. Make half a loop around Council Crest's east side; on the left is another Marquam Trail sign.

(continued on page 176)

3.95 miles : 8342 steps : IIIII difficulty : ◈ 45.509, -122.716

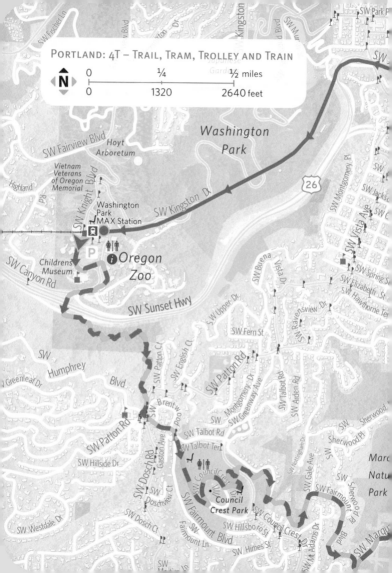

PORTLAND: 4T – TRAIL, TRAM, TROLLEY AND TRAIN

N

0	¼	½ miles
0	1320	2640 feet

SW Fischer Ln

SW Fairview Blvd

Kingston

SW Park Pl

SW Mu

Washington Park

Hoyt Arboretum

US 26

Vietnam Veterans of Oregon Memorial

Highland

SW Kingston Dr

SW Knight Blvd

Washington Park MAX Station

SW Montgomery Pl

SW Jacks

SW Vista Ave

SW C

SW Spring St

Childrens Museum

P

ⓘ Oregon Zoo

SW Canyon Rd

SW Elizabeth St

SW Hawthorne Ter

SW Buena Vista Dr

SW Sunset Hwy

SW Upper Dr

SW Fern St

SW Ravensview Dr

SW

Humphrey Blvd

W Greenleaf Dr

SW Patton Ct

SW English Ct

SW Patton Rd

SW Montgomery Dr

SW Greenway Ave

SW Talbot Rd

SW Arden Rd

Sherwood

Sherwood Pl

SW Patton Rd

Brentwood

SW Talbot Rd

SW Talbot Ter

SW Dosch Rd

Gaston Ave

SW

SW Northingham Dr

SW Gale Ave

SW Sherwood Dr

Marc

Natu

Park

SW Hillside Dr

SW Dosch Ct

Doschview Ct

SW

SW Council Crest

Council Crest Park

SW Hillsboro St

SW Council Crest Dr

SW M Adams Dr

SW Westdale Dr

SW Fairmount Blvd

Fairmount Ln

SW Himes St

SW Marq

BNB

Follow the trail downhill, following the Marquam Shelter-Terwilliger Trail sign.

Cross Greenway Avenue and stay on the trail. At the trail's intersection with Fairmount Boulevard, turn right onto Fairmount. Walk on the left side of the road, facing traffic. Turn left on Marquam Hill Road, which becomes Gibbs Street as it enters the Homestead neighborhood. OHSU's vast campus begins at Sam Jackson Park Road and U.S. Veterans Hospital Road. Cross here to get on the right side of Sam Jackson. Walk east to the tram.

Take the tram to the South Waterfront District. Disembark and walk to Moody and Gibbs. Here, catch the Portland Streetcar to 10th and Alder, then walk south on 10th to Morrison to catch a MAX train back to the start.

●　　●　　●

Portland Aerial Tram

Portland
Willamette Waterfront

This waterfront walk takes you on a loop through the heart of Portland, from downtown's riverfront to the booming Central Eastside and the popular Vera Katz Eastbank Esplanade. While the freeway noise is loud on the Esplanade, views are fabulous and on sunny days at lunchtime, the human scene is ever changing.

Start on the west side of the Willamette River at Governor Tom McCall Waterfront Park at SW Salmon Street and Naito Parkway. Walk north along the seawall, built after floods repeatedly ravaged downtown businesses. From 1940 to 1974, a freeway ran here.

Pass under the Morrison and Burnside bridges. At the Steel Bridge, take the bike/pedestrian path on the bridge's lower deck. The bridge, which dates from 1912, brings you to the 1.5-mile Eastbank Esplanade, with its 1,200-foot-long floating walkway. The walkway's concrete and steel sections were poured in Bellingham, Washington, trucked to Portland and floated into place. The walkway leads to dry land at Ash Street and to what was once a separate city, East Portland. Historic markers along the way provide interpretation of the waterfront scene. Walk south, passing under the Burnside and Morrison bridges and by mature plantings of native willow, alder, snowberry and roses.

Leave the Esplanade by taking the ramps or stairs up to the Hawthorne Bridge. Cross it to return to Waterfront Park. Head north to Salmon Street Springs, at the starting point.

2.6 miles : **5491** steps : ▌▌▌▌ difficulty : ◈ 45.515, -122.672

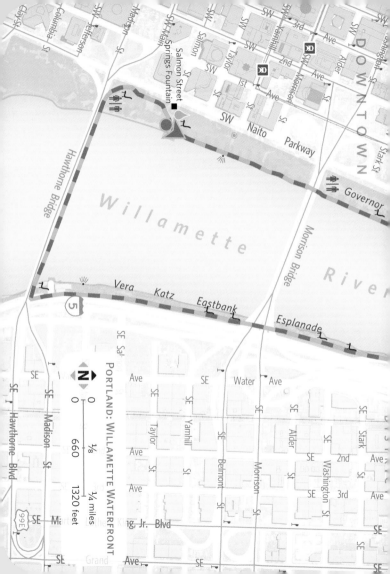

5th Ave

NW 6th Ave

C H I N A T O W N

NW 5th Ave

NW 4th Ave

NW Flanders St

NW 3rd Ave

NW Glisan St

NW Hoyt St

NW 3rd Ave

NW Irving St

Ave

SW 3rd Ave

W Burnside St

NW Ash St

O L D   T O W N

NW 2nd Ave

NW Davis St

NW Everett St

NW Naito Parkway

SW 2nd Ave

SW 1st Ave

NW Ankeny St

Saturday Market

NW 1st Ave

NW Couch St

SW Pine St

Naito Parkway

SW Front Ave

SW Couch St

Steel Bridge

Waterfront Park

Burnside Bridge

5

NE Occident St

NE Oregon St

C E N T R A L

SE Ash St

E Burnside St

NE 2nd Ave

NE 3rd Ave

NE Davis St

NE Glisan St

Convention Center

L L O Y D   D I S T R I C T

NE Hoyt

Ankeny St

99E

Luther King, Jr.

84

NE Martin Luther King Jr. Blvd

NE Couch St

Willamette River Bridges

The 187-mile Willamette River drains the 5,800 square miles of the Willamette Valley, one of the most fertile agricultural regions in the nation. In downtown Portland, the river is just 12 miles from its confluence with the Columbia River.

The Morrison Bridge opened in 1958 and replaced two earlier bridges, from 1887 and 1905. The 1887 bridge was the first to span the Willamette and replaced the Stark Street Ferry. The Burnside Bridge was built in 1926. During high water only, a bridge operator sits in the west tower. Other times of the year, the bridge is operated remotely, as is the Morrison. The Hawthorne Bridge is the state's busiest bike/pedestrian bridge. (Bridge facts courtesy of *The Portland Bridge Book* by Sharon Wood Wortman and Ed Wortman.)

Steel Bridge

Portland: Hillsdale to the River

This hilly walk in Portland's Southwest Hills combines several city staircases, forest paths and a river walk, with great views and significant elevation gain. You'll find plenty of places to eat along SW Macadam Avenue, which intersects the walk at about the halfway mark.

This route follows routes signed SW Trails 3 and SW Trails 4. Begin at Wilson High School's parking lot, SW Sunset Boulevard and Capitol Highway. Walk east through the lot to Burlingame Avenue. Walk downhill. Turn left on Burlingame Terrace. Carefully cross Terwilliger Boulevard and enter George Himes Park. Follow a trail downhill, passing underneath Barbur Boulevard and I-5.

Leave the park at Iowa Street, then turn right on Corbett. In one block, turn left on Carolina, then right on Virginia and left on Nebraska. Follow Nebraska to the riverside Willamette Park. Follow a paved park path to the right and exit the park at Miles Place. Turn right on Miles Street and cross Macadam. After crossing a street island, you're on Taylors Ferry Road. Begin climbing, following SW Trails 4 signs to a long staircase. Climb it; at the top continue straight on Custer. Turn right at Brier Place, then immediately left to walk on a road right-of-way adjacent to I-5. Walk the trail then go left to ascend a flight of stairs. At the top, turn right on 4th Avenue and take a quick left up more stairs. At the top, emerge on the right (east) side of Terwilliger. Turn right. At the stoplight at Terwilliger and Barbur, cross to get to Terwilliger's west side. Continue on Terwilliger north to Caldew. Turn left onto it; at 838, climb a set of stairs. At the top, go right on Burlingame to return to Wilson High School.

4.0 miles : 8,448 steps : ⚡ difficulty : ◈ 45.478, -122.692

PORTLAND: HILLSDALE TO THE RIVER

N

| 0 | 1/8 | 1/4 miles |

| 0 | 660 | 1320 feet |

Dewitt Park

SW Sunset Blvd

SW Capitol Hwy

SW Terwilliger Blvd Parkway

SW Capitol

George Himes Park

SW Terwilliger Pl

SW Burlingame Ave

SW Burlingame Pl

SW Burlingame Ter

SW Nebraska

Wilson Pool

Wilson HS

Rieke ES

SW Vermont St

SW Florida St

SW Terwilliger Blvd

HILLSDALE

SW 13th Ave

SW 14th Ave

SW Chestnut

SW 72nd Ave Dr

SW Texas St

SW 12th Dr

SW 11th Dr

SW 10th Ave

SW Burlingame Ave

SW 8th Ave

SW Chestnut St

SW 15th Ave

SW Nevada St

SW 13th Ave

SW Nevada Ter

SW 12th Ave

SW 7th Ave

SW 5th Ave

SW 4th Ave

SW Nev

SW Bertha Blvd

SW Caldew Dr

SW 13th Dr

SW Bertha Blvd

SW 13th Ave

SW Custer Dr

SW 17th Dr

SW Custer St

SW Canby St

SW Canby St

SW Terwilliger Blvd

SW Barbur Blvd

SW 5th Ave

5

SW Custer St

SW 4th Ave

SW 5th

Fu
Com
Ga
SW

Hillsdale's History

In 1851, John Slavin obtained a Donation Land Claim and built a cabin and barn at what is now Capitol Highway and Sunset Boulevard; Slavin's Road was later named Capitol Highway.

After the Northern Pacific rail line to Portland was complete, German, Swiss and Italian immigrants began to settle in Portland's Southwest hills, in what became known as Hillsdale. Many of them established dairies and vegetable farms. In 1890 the Raz brothers from Switzerland ran the Fulton Park Dairy, now the site of Wilson High School. It was a dairy until 1949.

● ● ●

Willamette Greenway riparian area

Portland
Portland Heights to Zoo

This walk combines stunning views of downtown and the Cascades, 19th century homes, wooded paths and a ride on Portland's only subway. Stop for a snack at Strohecker's Grocery on your way to an afternoon visiting the animals at the Oregon Zoo.

From SW 18th Avenue and Jefferson Street, walk south on 18th, passing underneath Highway 26. Immediately after the tunnel, turn left on an asphalt path. Turn right onto 16th Avenue and then right on Montgomery, which winds uphill. Take a stairway on the left that leads up to Vista Avenue. At the top of the stairs, turn left on Vista, then left on Jackson. Turn right on 18th, a steep street along which a cable car operated in the 1890s. Follow 18th to Spring Street, named after the spring that once fed the neighborhood fire station. Turn right on Spring and pass the fire station, Ainsworth School and the Ainsworth Greenspace, with its 60-meter-long pedestrian bridge.

Emerge from the bridge onto St. Helens Court, turn right and then left onto Montgomery Drive. After 0.5 mile, turn right on Patton Road, passing Strohecker's. In business over 100 years, it specializes in rare and gourmet foods. Across from Heather Lane, turn right off Patton onto the Marquam Trail. Follow it through the woods and across Highway 26 to the zoo.

After visiting the zoo, head to the Washington Park MAX station; the elevator drops you 260 feet to the deepest transit station in North America. Take the train east one stop to the starting point.

5.6 miles ⋮ **11,756** steps ⋮ ▁▃▅▇ difficulty ⋮ ◀◉▶ 45.517, -122.692

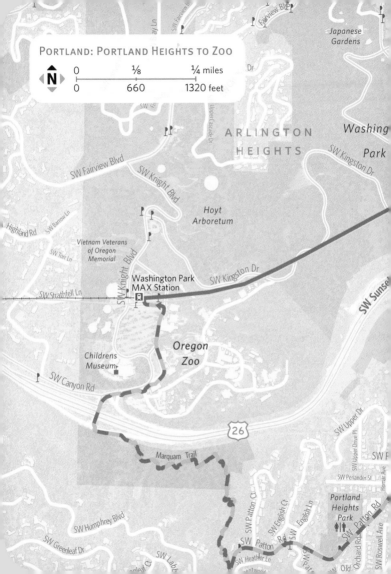

PORTLAND: PORTLAND HEIGHTS TO ZOO

N

| 0 | ⅛ | ¼ miles |
| 0 | 660 | 1320 feet |

Japanese Gardens

ARLINGTON HEIGHTS

Washington Park

SW Kingston Dr

SW Fairview Blvd

SW Knight Blvd

Upper Cascade Dr

Hoyt Arboretum

SW Knight Blvd

SW Kingston Dr

Highland Rd

SW Barrow Ln

SW Torr Ln

Vietnam Veterans of Oregon Memorial

Washington Park MAX Station

SW Strathfell Ln

SW Sunset

Childrens Museum

Oregon Zoo

SW Canyon Rd

26

Marquam Trail

SW Upper Dr

SW Upper Drive Pl

SW F

SW Periander St

Portland Heights Park

SW Humphrey Blvd

SW Greenleaf Dr

SW Patton Ct

SW English Ct

SW English Ct

SW Patton Rd

SW Patton Rd

SW Old Orchard Rd

SW Roswell Ave

SW Heather Ln

SW Lab

SW Canyon Rd
SW 20th
SW
Main St
SW 18th Ave
SW Sa

GOOSE HOLLOW

Madison St

Lincoln HS

SW Jefferson St
SW Prospect Dr

Goose Hollow
MAX Station

SW Jefferson St
SW 16th Ave
SW 14th

SW Market Street Dr

SW 17th Ave
SW Columbia St

SW 18th Ave
SW Clay St

SW Market St

SW Mill Street Ter

SW Montgomery St
SW Montgomery St

US 26

SW Montgomery Pl

SW Montgomery Dr

SW Carter Ln

SW 18th Ave

SW Harrison St

SW Upper Hall St
SW 18th Ave
SW Hall St

405

SW 21st
SW Montgomery

SW Jackson St

SW Carter Ln

SW College St

SW 13th Ave

SW Cardinell Dr

SOUTHWEST

SW Vista Ave

SW Clifton
St

SW 19th Ave

HILLS

SW 18th Ave

SW 17th Ave

SW Myrtle St

21st Ave

SW
Laurel St

SW Elm St

SW 15th Ave

SW Cardinell Dr

SW Clifto

SW Myrtle Dr

SW Rivington C

Ainsworth
ES

SW St Helens Ct

SW Spring St

SW 17th Ave

SW 16th Ave

SW Cardinell Ave

SW Vista Ave

SW Myrtle Dr

SW Buckingham

SW Elizabeth St

SW Hawthorne Ter

Ravensview Dr

SW High St

Governors
Park

SW Davenport St

SW Chelmsford Ave

SW Gerald Ave

SW Terrace Dr

SW BraeMar Ct

SW Broadway Dr

Broadway Dr

SW Arden Rd

SW Talbot Rd

SW Davenport Dr

Marquam
Nature Park

A Ride to the Top

Predecessors of electric streetcars, cable cars were powered by cables that pulled cars along the tracks, making them ideal for hilly terrain. The Portland Heights Cable Car line was built in 1887 along Chapman Street (now 18th Avenue). It started near today's Goose Hollow MAX station and climbed the hill via a wooden trestle built over the ravine at Montgomery Drive and Cable Avenue. Cars traveled 1,000 feet at a 20 percent grade to Jackson Street, where the line continued on grade to its turnaround on Spring Street. The trestle was torn down in 1903 after several runaway crashes. Service was replaced by the Council Crest streetcar, which carried passengers over the newly constructed Vista Bridge. That line ran until the 1950s.

Polar Bears at the Oregon Zoo

Portland
South Portland

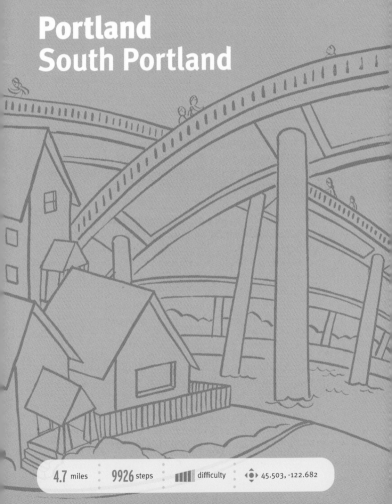

4.7 miles : 9926 steps : ▮▮▮▮ difficulty : ◈ 45.503, -122.682

This long walk explores historic South Portland, site of im-migrant Jewish and Italian communities in the early 1900s, and then loops back along the Willamette Greenway Trail and into the evolving South Waterfront District. Along the way are parks, beautiful 19th century homes, quiet streets and views of Ross Island.

Begin at SW Barbur Boulevard and Sheridan Street at Duniway Park, a park built in 1918 on landfill over a creek valley that had become the city dump. Walk to the south end of the running track, next to the YMCA, and take the hiking trail climbing into the woods. At a T inter-section, keep left to continue climbing the steep trail, which emerges onto Terwilliger Boulevard, a roadway/walking path dedicated in 1912 as part of the city's intended chain of scenic parkways.

Turn left on Terwilliger and walk past OHSU. Make what will be the first of four passes under the aerial tram. Turn left on an asphalt path marked with a SW Trails 1 sign. Follow it downhill to Barbur, passing private homes. Turn left on Barbur, which follows a railroad alignment from the 1860s. In the 1930s, the rail line was abandoned. Walk to the stoplight at Hooker and cross Barbur. Walk east on Hooker. On the right is Lair Hill Park, once the site of a large mansion that became the first county hospital. A Carnegie library sits at 2nd and Hooker behind a heritage copper beech.

Turn left on 2nd and right on Meade. In the southeast corner, Kesser Israel was the last of the original Jewish synagogues that served newly immigrated eastern European Jews from the 1890s onward. It left South Portland in 2006.

From Meade, turn right on 1st, route of the city's first horse-drawn trolley. Walk south to Grover, turn left, walk under the elevated Naito Parkway and then turn right on Water Avenue. Pass the Water/Gibbs

Community Garden and many fine old Queen Anne homes. Turn left on Curry, then right on Corbett. Walk south about 0.8 mile on this street where homes range from the earliest days of South Portland to the newest 21st century condominiums.

From Corbett, turn left on Boundary. Cross Macadam at a stoplight, then turn left on Landing Drive, using caution as there is no sidewalk here. Turn right onto a sidewalk marked by two concrete stanchions. It leads to the Heron Point Wetland on the Willamette Greenway Trail. Watch for bicyclists as you turn left to walk along the river. Ross Island views are superb here.

Just past the lovely Cottonwood Bay Natural Area, the trail ends. Turn left and then right to walk on a multiuse path along railroad tracks. At Bancroft Street is the Willamette Shore Trolley station. During warm weather, an excursion train runs south to downtown Lake Oswego. North of Bancroft, walk along Moody Avenue in the South Waterfront District. Sidewalk bioswales catch and filter street and roof run-off through the soil rather than directing it into the sewer system. In 2010, a pedestrian bridge will connect this area with South Portland along the Gibbs Street alignment.

(continued on page 194)

Cyclists on the Willamette Greenway

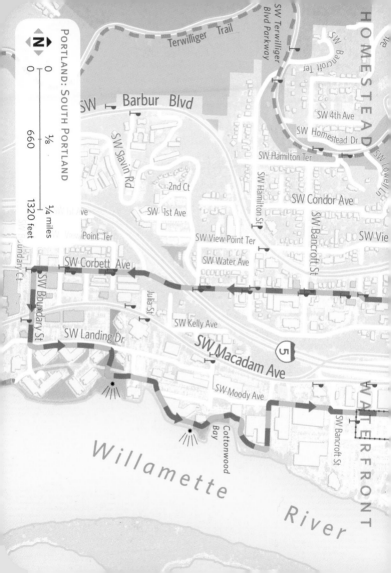

N

0
0

1/8
660

1/4 miles
1320 feet

SW Terwilliger Blvd Parkway

SW Terwilliger Trail

Terwilliger Trail

SW Bancroft Ter

HOMESTEAD

SW Barbur Blvd

SW 4th Ave

SW Homestead Dr

SW Slavin Rd

SW Hamilton Ter

SW Lowell St

2nd Ct

SW 1st Ave

SW Hamilton St

SW Condor Ave

View Point Ter

SW View Point Ter

SW Bancroft St

SW Vie

SW Corbett Ave

SW Water Ave

SW Boundary St

Julia St

SW Kelly Ave

SW Landing Dr

SW Macadam Ave

5

SW Moody Ave

Cottonwood Bay

SW Bancroft St

WATERFRONT

Willamette River

Turn left off Moody onto Sheridan, under the soaring approach to the Marquam Bridge. From Sheridan, turn left onto Water (which becomes Corbett), then right at Arthur. Old homes here are remnants of the once thriving immigrant Italian and Jewish neighborhood, much of which was razed for roadway and urban renewal projects.

At a ramp for Naito Parkway, turn left and descend stairs to a New York style underground passage that runs under Arthur. (If the passageway is beyond your comfort level, walk west one block to the light at 1st Avenue and then back east along the south side of Arthur.) Once on the south side of Arthur, walk south along Kelly/Naito. In one block, at Hooker, walk half a block and climb the ramp to a pedestrian walkway over Naito. Formerly called Front Avenue, this is a street turned into an expressway in the 1940s, following recommendations of New York urban planner Robert Moses, a proponent of highways over mass transit. Once off the walkway, continue west on Hooker. Cross Barbur at the light, turn right and return to Duniway Park.

1886 apartment building

Beaverton
Downtown to Round

Beaverton, a former farming village, is now the fifth largest Oregon city and home to one of the area's most popular farmers markets. On this 1.4-mile (one-way) walk, stroll under hanging flower baskets and through City Park in downtown Beaverton on the way to Beaverton Round, a mix of shops, offices, restaurants and lofts at the Beaverton Central MAX station.

Begin at Beaverton City Library, SW 5th Street and Hall Boulevard. Cross Hall to City Park, with its playground, restrooms, fountains and picnic tables under tall pines. Next to the park on Hall Boulevard is the seasonal Beaverton Farmers Market.

From the park, walk west on 4th and turn right onto Watson. At 2nd, turn left and then right onto Angel Avenue. At 2nd and Angel, listen for red breasted nuthatches in a huge oak. From Angel, turn right on 1st, walk three blocks and turn right on Hall and then left on 2nd. At Lombard, turn left and cross Farmington Road.

Turn left onto Broadway and follow it into the Downtown Beaverton Historic District, which is on the National Register of Historic Places. Here, shops and cafes invite you to linger. Turn right onto Watson and cross Canyon Road, once the route used by local farmers to haul produce into Portland. After crossing the MAX tracks, turn left into The Round, where a plaza, grassy park area and waterfall create an urban oasis on the former site of a horseradish farm.

2.8 miles ⋮ **5914** steps ⋮ ▮▮▮▮ difficulty ⋮ ◈ 45.483, -122.804

SW Angel Ave

SW 4th St

SW Watson Ave

SW 5th St

City
Park

SW 3rd St

SW Washington Ave

P

SW 2nd St

SW 1st St

SW Hall Blvd

Library
Green

B E A V E R T O N

Beaverton
Central Library

SW Tucker Ave

10

SW Farmington Rd

SW Betts Ave

SW Franklin Ave

Post
Office

SW Chapman Ave

SW Franklin Ave

SW 2nd St

SW Lombard Ave

N

BEAVERTON: DOWNTOWN TO ROUND

0   0
0

1/16

330

1/8 miles

660 feet

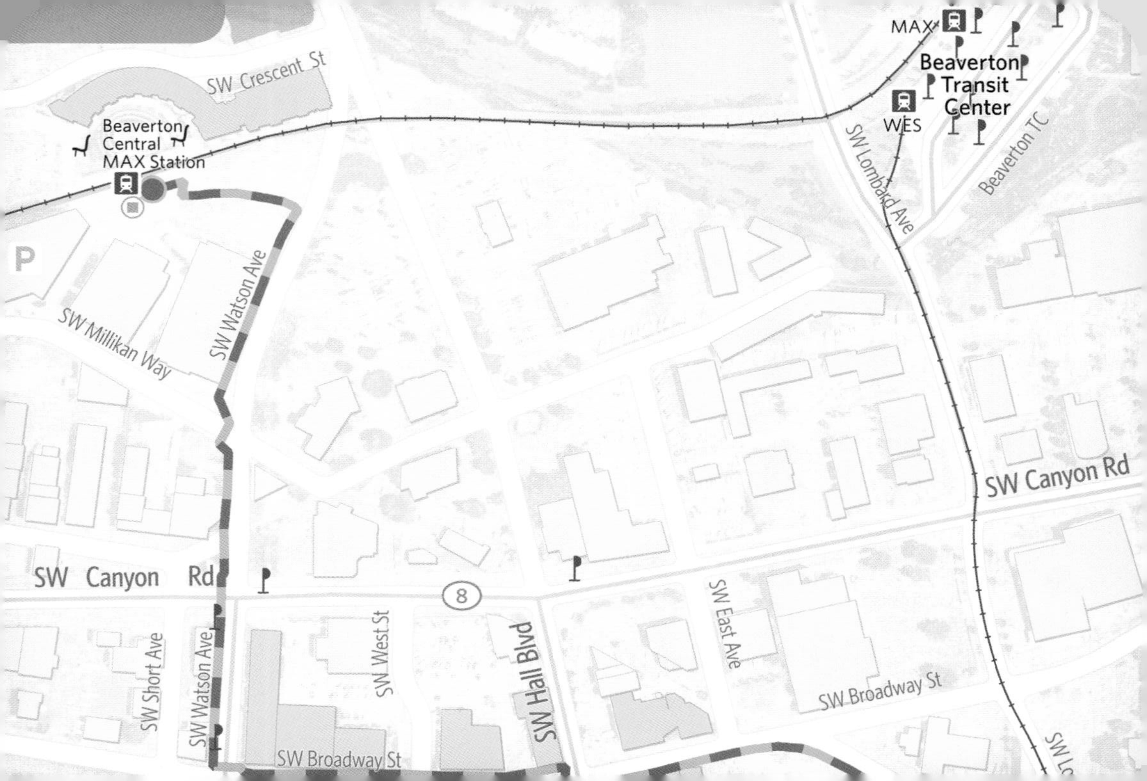

SW Crescent St
Beaverton Central MAX Station
P
SW Millikan Way
SW Watson Ave
MAX
Beaverton Transit Center
WES
SW Lombard Ave
Beaverton TC
SW Canyon Rd
8
SW Short Ave
SW Watson Ave
SW West St
SW Hall Blvd
SW East Ave
SW Broadway St
SW Broadway St
SW Canyon Rd

The Beaverton Farmers Market

Native peoples called the area now known as Beaverton "Chakeipi," for "place of the beaver." Early settlers called it Beaver Dam. They settled on the high ground of the dams, above swampy areas engineered for millennia by beavers. Once drained, the ground was excellent for growing onions and other produce.

The Beaverton Farmers Market, the largest agriculture-only farmers market in the Northwest, features cheeses, produce, meats and plants from the Tualatin and Willamette valleys. On summer Saturdays, over 15,000 people come to buy local products from 100 vendors and enjoy live music and the fountain in the adjacent City Park. The market is open Saturdays, mid-May to late October, 8 a.m. to 1:30 p.m. and Wednesdays, mid-June to late August, 10 a.m. to 2 p.m. Visit www.beavertonfarmersmarket.com for more information.

● ● ●

Beaverton Farmers Market

Forest Grove
Pacific University and Clark Historic District

2.4 miles : 5069 steps : difficulty : 45.519, -123.111

This walk passes through Pacific University's campus on to the 1890s brick storefronts in downtown Forest Grove and into the Clark Historic District, where homes date from the 1850s. Along the way are many of the state's oldest giant sequoias.

Note: For a printable map and list of historic buildings seen on this walk, visit www.forestgrove-or.gov/city-government/historic-landmarks-board-walking-tour.html

Pacific University campus

Forest Grove, a town of 20,000, sits scenically where the Tualatin Plains transition into the Coast Range. The town owes its existence to Pacific University, founded as a prep school and college in 1849 by Congregationalists and today a thriving university of 2,500 students, tucked into a woodsy setting adjacent to downtown Forest Grove.

From the starting point at College Way and Pacific Avenue, walk north to Pacific University's Old College Hall, the oldest structure on campus, dating from 1850. For 40 years, it was the school's sole building. Walk to the campus side of Old College Hall; on the right is Carnegie Hall, a college library built in 1912. On the diagonal walkway, head toward the imposing red brick Marsh Hall, the heart of the campus, built in 1895. Fire gutted it in 1975 but it was rebuilt and houses the school's administrative functions. From Marsh Hall, walk west on the walkway toward 21st Avenue, passing an intriguing petrified stump. At 2019 21st is the Propstra Creamery building, given to Pacific University by Helen Propstra, whose parents once operated a creamery in town.

From 21st, turn left on Main and enjoy its shops and restaurants. Walk south on Main through downtown, passing into the Clark Historic District at about 18th Avenue. The district is named for Harvey Clark, who owned this land and in 1849 donated it to the school as an endowment, with hopes that its 1-acre lots would sell to fund the school's growth.

Pass the 1931 Central School, decommissioned after the 1993 Scott's Mill earthquake. From Main, turn left on 17th and then right on Ash. At 15th is a lovely view of the Tualatin River floodplain to the south. Turn left on 15th and left on Birch. At 1604 Birch is the 1859 Thomas Hines home, a simple Classical Revival style, typical of frame homes built on the Tualatin Plains when settlers were ready to step up from a log cabin.

From Birch, turn right on 16th and left on Cedar. Take Cedar up to 19th, turn right and pass the 1873 Cornelius House at 2314 19th, named for Benjamin Cornelius, who helped locate a southern immigrant route to Oregon in the 1840s. His son Thomas founded Cornelius, Oregon.

From 19th, turn left on Elm and then left on Pacific and walk two blocks. The campus is on your right. Meander back to the starting point via campus walkways. Don't miss the new library, with its great blend of art and function. The second floor mezzanine, with its view into the campus tree canopy, is a splendid place to rest after a walk.

Fall color in Forest Grove

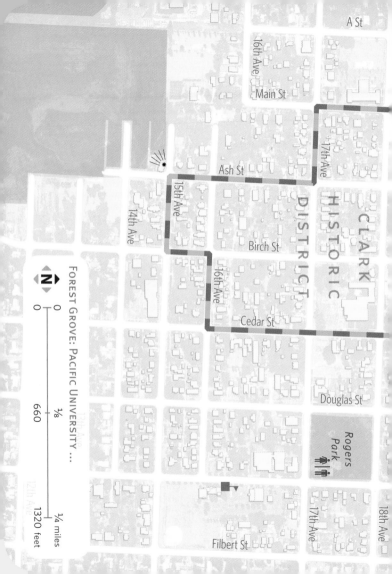

FOREST GROVE: PACIFIC UNIVERSITY ...

N

0 ——— 0 ——— 660 ——— 1320 feet
    ⅛   ¼ miles

A St

16th Ave

Main St

17th Ave

Ash St

15th Ave

14th Ave

Birch St

CLARK HISTORIC DISTRICT

16th Ave

Cedar St

Douglas St

Rogers Park

17th Ave

18th Ave

Filbert St

12th Ave

The Sequoia Story

The many giant sequoias seen on the walk are specimens of the largest tree species on earth, *sequoiadendron giganteum*. Washington County's old giant sequoias are attributed to nurseryman John R. Porter, who moved to Oregon from Ohio in 1847 and opened a nursery in Hillsboro. He went south to prospect for gold during the 1849 California Gold Rush and rode back to Oregon, not with gold in his saddlebags but with cones of the giant sequoia. He cultivated the seeds and began planting them in Washington County. Many of the seedlings cultivated in his nursery tower over Forest Grove streets. The Oregon Department of Forestry lists two of them on its Register of Big Trees. Both are a few blocks off the route, but worth a look: at 1651 Hawthorne and at B Street and Pacific Avenue. Other sequoias from Porter's nursery are still growing tall at the Washington County Courthouse in Hillsboro.

Pacific University campus

Hillsboro
Downtown

Hillsboro, once a sleepy agricultural town, has a beautiful historic downtown with a strong emphasis on the arts and a hometown ambience. This and other amenities caused U.S. News and World Report to name Hillsboro one of its top 10 places to retire. This 1.2-mile (one-way) walk explores the charms and art scene of downtown Hillsboro.

Take the Blue Line MAX to its terminus at Main Street and Adams Avenue. Exit MAX, turn right and walk along Main Street. Cross 1st. On the left is the Washington County Courthouse, framed by giant sequoias. Here, on summer Saturdays is the Hillsboro Farmers Market. Main Street is a great place to explore old storefronts, many of which house tempting antique shops.

From Main, turn right at 2nd. HART (Hillsboro Artists' Regional Theater) is on the right. Turn left onto Washington and then left onto 3rd. At Main, turn left to enjoy the Venetian Theatre and Bistro in the renovated Town Theater.

From the theater, walk east on Main to 5th. In the northeast corner is the Glenn and Viola Walters Cultural Arts Center, opened in 2004 in a former Lutheran church. Inside are classrooms, galleries, offices of art organizations and performance space.

Continue east on Main past historic homes. Turn right on 9th, walk one block and turn right on Washington. Walk one block to 8th. Look south to Tuality Hospital, the largest employer in downtown Hillsboro. End the walk by continuing west to the Tuality Hospital/SE 8th Avenue MAX stop.

2.4 miles : **5069** steps : difficulty : 45.522, -122.991

NW Jackson St

Bagley
Park

NW Adams Ave

N 1st Ave

NW Lincoln St

Washington
County Law
Library

NE 2nd Ave

NE 3rd Ave

NE 4th Ave

Washington
County
Courthouse

W Main St

Hatfield Govt
Center
MAX Station

Hillsboro
Civic
Center

Hillsboro TC

SW Washington St

Hillsboro
Central/SE 3rd
MAX Station

SW Adams Ave

S 1st Ave

P

SE 2nd Ave

SE 3rd Ave

SE 4th Ave

SW Baseline St

HILLSBORO: DOWNTOWN

N

0   1/16   1/8 miles

0   330   660 feet

SW Oak

St.
Matthew
ES

Hillsboro History

Hillsboro is named for David Hill, an Oregon Trail pioneer. He named the area on his donation land claim Columbus but it was renamed Hillsborough on his death in 1850. In 1876, when the city incorporated, the name became Hillsboro.

The giant sequoias at the Washington County Courthouse came from Porter & Sons Nursery. Cones from California had been brought to Oregon by John Porter after his stint in gold-mining country. Originally eight were planted at the courthouse in 1880. Five survive.

The stone for the Walters Cultural Art Center was quarried in the 1940s by congregation members, who hauled the rock in 150 trips from Camas, Washington to Hillsboro. The center is named for the founders of the Glenn Walters Nursery, Oregon's largest nursery, with 18 farms in Washington County.

● ● ●

Walters Community Art Center

Hillsboro
Rock Creek Trail

This 1.6-mile (one-way) paved trail extends north from Orchard Park to Rock Creek Boulevard. While occasionally skirting residential and corporate complexes, it follows Rock Creek and provides a natural escape within the city. Combine this walk with an additional mile of paved trail and wetland boardwalks within the 21-acre Orchard Park.

Begin at the Orchard Park parking lot (20900 NW Amberwood Drive). Turn right on Amberwood, walk east to 206th, cross Amberwood and walk west on it to the Rock Creek Trail sign. Follow the trail along Rock Creek, enjoying native vegetation and wildlife. At Cornell, again walk to 206th to cross, and then walk west on Cornell to the trail's continuation. The trail passes under the Sunset Highway and through towering evergreens to Rock Creek Park. Return on the same path.

Points of interest include hundreds of native trees and shrubs planted by Hillsboro Parks and Recreation staff and volunteers to maintain a healthy watershed. Invasive species are removed regularly to ensure that these native species can thrive. Habitat enhancement features such as swallow and duck houses have also been installed. Ducks are frequently seen along the trail and a great blue heron rookery is just north of Evergreen Parkway. A memorial bench also provides a place to rest or just enjoy the scenery.

This is a paved ADA accessible trail, with some boardwalk sections. Parts of the trail may be closed during periods of high water. Orchard Park offers restrooms and picnicking.

 3.2 miles : 6758 steps : difficulty : 45.536, -122.891

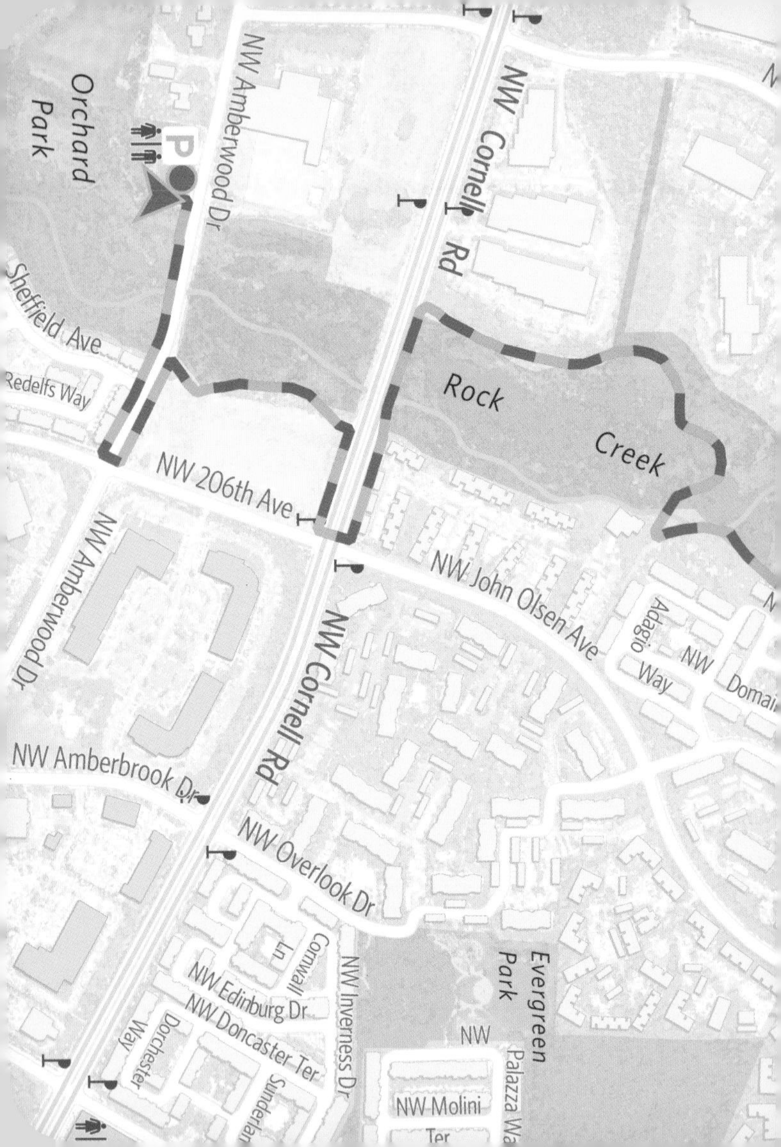

Orchard Park

NW Amberwood Dr

NW Cornell Rd

Sheffield Ave

Redelfs Way

NW 206th Ave

Rock

Creek

NW Amberwood Dr

NW John Olsen Ave

Adagio Way

NW Domai

NW Cornell Rd

NW Amberbrook Dr

NW Overlook Dr

Cornwall Ln

NW Inverness Dr

Evergreen Park

Palazza Wa

NW Edinburg Dr

NW Doncaster Ter

Dorchester Way

Sunderlan

NW

NW Molini Ter

N

0
0

⅛
660

¼ miles
1320 feet

26

NW 211th Ter

NW Aloclek Pl

NW Evergreen Pky

Greenway

NW Evergreen Pky

NW Tanasbourne Dr

NW Landsbourne Dr

NW John Olsen

Sunset Hwy

Rock Creek Park

NW Rock Creek Blvd

Rock Creek Country Club

NW Rock Creek D

Dr

An Escape in the City

The Hillsboro Parks and Recreation department began work on the Rock Creek Trail in 1998. With the assistance of voter-approved natural areas bond measure funds from Metro, the trail is now 1.6 miles long, connecting residential, commercial and industrial neighborhoods as it follows Rock Creek. Flowing out of the Tualatin Mountains to the north, Rock Creek flows into the Tualatin River at Rood Bridge Park in south Hillsboro and eventually into the Willamette River. It is one of 89 Rock Creeks in Oregon. This Rock Creek's watershed drains about 65 square miles and is home to various waterfowl, fish and other wildlife. The city's long-range plan calls for the Rock Creek Trail to extend more than 6 miles.

Boardwalk over wetlands

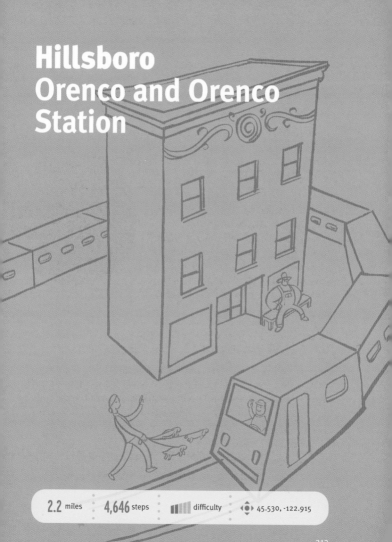

Hillsboro
Orenco and Orenco Station

2.2 miles · 4,646 steps · ▮▮▮▮ difficulty · ◈ 45.530, -122.915

This walk takes you through two planned communities, one old, one new: the 1906 town of Orenco, formed by the Oregon Nursery Company, and Orenco Station, an experiment in the New Urbanism created in 1997. In 2006, Sunset magazine named Orenco Station the West Coast's best new suburb.

From the MAX stop, walk east to a sidewalk on the south side of the tracks. Take it to 231st Avenue and turn right. Walk half a block and turn left on NW Alder Street into old Orenco.

Barn near Orenco Station

In 1906, Archibald McGill and Malcolm McDonald bought 1,200 acres for their new Oregon Nursery Company. Fifty horses tilled fields where fruit and shade trees were soon planted. A 2-acre packing shed was located just north of what are now the MAX tracks. The town's name is a contraction of the company's name; it incorporated in 1913 with about 500 residents, many immigrants from Hungary. The company thrived until the 1910s, when it planted one million trees with plans to export apples to Europe. World War I laid waste to that plan. By 1927, the company was bankrupt.

At 22930 is the 1908 Orenco Grocery/Mercantile. At 22870 is Orenco Drug, where the town doctor practiced and dispensed medicine. Across from it was the depot of the Oregon Electric Rail; the tracks were laid in 1908. Their alignment is used by the MAX trains. Other businesses along Alder were a hotel, dry goods store, grocery, boarding houses, hardware store, blacksmith, livery and a printing shop

From Alder, turn right onto 228th. Ahead is the 1911 Orenco Presbyterian Church. Turn left onto Birch and follow it to just beyond Orenco

Elementary, where you can see the old nursery grounds. In 1953, a golf course opened here. In 2005, it closed and the land was sold to a home developer. Retrace your steps on Birch to 229th; turn left and then right on Chestnut, walking under Orenco's century-old elms that have created a sheltered nook amid the bustle of modern Washington County.

Leave the past behind when you cross 231st into a new neighborhood. Turn right at 62nd, right at Alder and then immediately left into a small courtyard to cross the train tracks. Once beyond the tracks, veer a bit left to walk north on Orenco Station Parkway.

Cross Cornell Road and enter Orenco Station's town center. As you walk north to Central Park, restaurants, stores and live/work units blend into duplexes and single family homes, with alleys to keep cars out of sight.

Turn right at Brighton, left at 63rd and left at Rosebay Drive. Come back to the park and walk down its west side to Brighton. Turn right and then left onto 61st where the Orenco Station Farmers Market is held Sundays, mid May through mid October, 10 a.m. to 2 p.m., in the parking lot next to New Seasons.

Return by walking down Orenco Station Parkway to the MAX stop.

Orenco Grocery/Mercantile

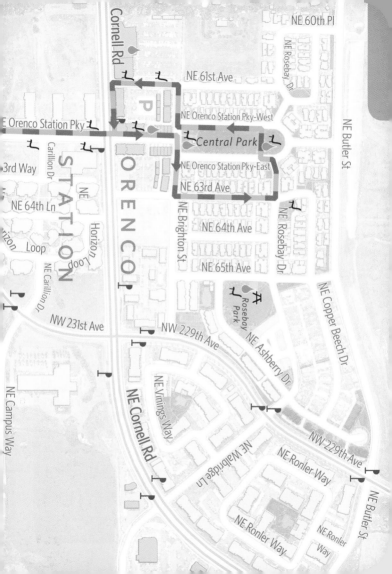

The Orenco Station Story

Orenco Station, constructed out of agricultural land in the 1990s and nearing completion a decade later, is an example of the New Urbanism, an urban design movement that emphasizes a sense of place. Principles of the New Urbanism include walkability, with shopping, jobs and recreation less than a 10-minute walk away; and a hierarchy of narrow streets, boulevards and alleys in a pedestrian-friendly design. Other hallmarks include a diversity of building types (commercial and residential), diversity of residents' ages, income levels and cultures, and an emphasis on beauty and aesthetically pleasing design.

Seen in Orenco Station are other principles of the movement: a traditional neighborhood structure, with a discernible center and public spaces and with higher housing densities at the center and progressively less density toward the edge; and a connection to alternative transportation (in this case, the light rail line), in order to minimize the site's and residents' environmental impacts.

●　　●　　●

Orenco Station

Tigard
Fanno Creek Greenway Trail

The Fanno Creek Greenway Trail connects communities in the metro region from Portland to Durham. This 2.7-mile section of the trail in Tigard offers great views of the creek as it meanders through three city parks and other natural areas preserved to promote the creek's floodplain and wetlands. These areas provide great habitat for coyotes, turtles and red-tailed hawks.

Follow the Greenway Trail south from Beaverton under Scholls Ferry Road or begin at a path next to 11338 Ironwood Drive in Tigard and turn right on the asphalt trail. Walk south through Englewood Park. Cross North Dakota Street, continuing south on the trail. Cross Tigard Street and follow the trail to Tiedeman Avenue. Turn left onto Tiedeman, walk 400 feet to the asphalt trail in Woodard Park and turn right. Follow the trail to Johnson Street. Turn left and walk to Highway 99. Cross at Main Street, where you can find places to eat and drink in the heart of Tigard.

Walk north on Main. As you cross Fanno Creek, follow signs into Fanno Creek Park. Stay east on the main trail which ends at Hall Boulevard. Nearby is the Tigard Civic Center with City Hall, the Police Station and the Jim Griffith Memorial Skatepark. A block south on Hall is the Tigard Library. A planned connecting trail across Hall will lead past the library south to Fanno Creek Drive.

Retrace your steps to the starting point.

5.4 miles : 11405 steps : ▮▮▮▮ difficulty : ◈ 45.446, -122.791

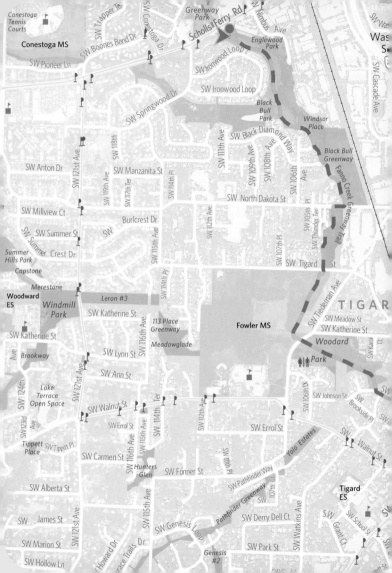

TIGARD: FANNO CREEK GREENWAY TRAIL

N

0	¼	½ miles
0	1320	2640 feet

Restoring Nature

Fanno Creek for about 1 mile south of Scholls Ferry Road has been intensively restored, with native plantings by Fans of Fanno and stream realignment (to create meanders) by Clean Water Services. Ash and Hiteon creeks and other small streams flow into Fanno Creek along this stretch. Seagoing cutthroat trout and steelhead are seen here.

Woodard Park's 11 acres are best known for their spreading Oregon white oaks and tall ponderosa pines. Park structures were designed around the trees. Half the park was purchased by Metro with voter-approved natural areas bond measure funds in 1999.

Fanno Creek Park's 30 acres consist of wooded and open areas, floodplain and small ponds. Two of the four foot bridges spanning Fanno Creek were made from old flatbed rail cars. The park has been cleared of non-native Himalayan blackberry and replanted with native trees and shrubs, and more restoration and stream work are planned.

Crossing the creek

Beaverton
Fanno Creek Greenway Trail

Two walks on the Fanno Creek Greenway Trail showcase the creek along which early settlers made their claims. The first walk crosses Fanno Creek while following the former route of the Oregon Electric Railroad in unincorporated Washington County. The second walk closely follows Fanno Creek as it meanders south through Beaverton.

Route One

[**2.3** miles   **4942** steps   ▮▮▯▯ difficulty   ◈ 45.467, -122.752]

For the Oregon Electric Railroad section, begin at the Garden Home Recreation Center, 7475 SW Oleson Road. The paved multiuse trail begins north of the parking lot. Follow it west 1.15 mile to its end at 92nd Avenue. It passes peaceful Garden Home streets on the left and the Portland Golf Club on the right, which occupies lowlands of marshes and ponds adjacent to the creek. Vista Brook Park offers a place to picnic and watch ducks in a small pond. At 92nd Avenue, turn around and retrace your steps to the start.

Route Two

[**3.6** miles   **7603** steps   ▮▮▮▯ difficulty   ◈ 45.469, -122.790]

For this 1.8-mile (one-way) section, begin at SW Denney Road just west of Highway 217. The trailhead offers parking, a bike rack and an information kiosk. Walk south on the paved path. Fanno Creek flows westerly from its headwaters in Portland's Hillsdale neighborhood to its confluence with the Tualatin River in Durham. Watch for groves of Oregon ash and water birds such as the great blue heron. At Hall Boulevard, head a half block west, cross Hall at

(continued on page 226)

SW Old Scholls Ferry Rd
SW Scholls Ferry Rd
SW 86th Ave
SW 90th Ave
Vista Brook Park
SW becker Dr
SW Oak Ln
SW Bohmann Pky
Fanno Creek Trail at Oregon Electric ROW

Portland Golf Club

Oregon Episcopal School
SW Nicol Rd
Montclair ES
SW Oleson Rd
SW Peyton Rd
Arranmore Open Space
Arranmore Way
SW Miles Ct

Hideaway Park

SW Hunt Club Dr
SW Hunt Club Ln
Aloma Way
SW Oleson Ave
SW Canby St

Rd

SW Rambler Ln
SW 90th Ave
SW 87th Ave
SW 84th Ave
SW 83rd Ave
SW 82nd Ave
SW 81st Ave
SW 78th Ave
SW 77th Ave
SW 76th Ave

SW Oleson Ave
SW 70th Ave
SW 69th Ave
SW 68th Ave
SW Multnomah Blvd
SW 62nd Pl

SW Garden Home Rd

SW 87th Ave
SW Dolph St
SW Obrien St
SW Shirley Ln
SW Stewart St
SW Mayo St

SW 69th Ave
SW 67th Ave
SW 66th Ave
SW Mayo St
SW Dolph Dr
SW Dolph D

Garden Home Park
SW 99th Ave
SW Alden St
SW Oleson Rd
SW Alden St
SW 71st Ave
Moonshadow Park

SW 80th Ave
SW Greenwood Dr
SW 74th Ave
SW Ashdale Dr
SW Orchid St

SW 89th Ave
SW 90th Ave
SW Leslie St
SW Leslie St
SW Lara St
SW Florence Ln
SW 71st Ter
SW Brugger S

SW 91st Ave
SW 82nd Ave
SW Birch St
Taylors Creek Park
SW 75th Ave
SW Taylors Ferry Rd
SW 69th Ave
SW 65th Ave
SW 62nd Ave

SW Cedarcrest St

W Borders St
SW 90th Ave
SW Washington Dr
SW 82nd Ave
SW Larch St
SW Landau St
SW 27th Ave
SW Landau St
SW Ventura Dr
SW 72nd Ave

Metzger Park
SW Hall Blvd
SW Locust St

BEAVERTON: FANNO CREEK GREENWAY TRAIL

N

| 0 | ¼ | ½ miles |
| 0 | 1320 | 2640 feet |

the light, then head a half block east to access the next trail segment in Greenway Park. South of Hall, on Creekside Place, visit the 1857 Augustus Fanno farmhouse (open by appointment only). At Scholls Ferry Road, the boundary between Beaverton and Tigard, retrace your steps to the start.

The Fanno Story

Augustus Fanno arrived in Oregon in 1846. Soon after, his wife and newborn child died in Linn City (a former town across the Willamette River from Oregon City). Fanno left Linn City, following an Indian trail into the Tualatin Plains, where he claimed land on a creek (now Fanno Creek). The trail Fanno followed later became known as the Astoria-Military Road. He chose his claim's location so he could sell produce to travelers on the trail. His first home, made of logs, was built in 1851; the current home, reflecting his agricultural success, was built in 1857. Fanno was a pioneer onion grower in the Tualatin Valley; at the 1905 Lewis and Clark Exposition in Portland, he was proclaimed the "Onion King." The Fanno family farmed onions along the creek until about 1940 when onion maggots decimated their crops. (Information courtesy of Virginia Mapes's *Chakeipi: The Place of the Beaver*.)

●　●　●

Aerial view of Fanno Creek

More Great Places to Walk

Forest Park and Wildwood Trail
Portland

The 30-mile Wildwood Trail passes through some of the most pristine natural areas in the region as it traverses Northwest Portland's 5,157 acre Forest Park. The Wildwood connects to dozens of shorter trails within the park and is linked to the greater regional trail network. Attractions along the trail include the Vietnam Veterans Memorial, Hoyt Arboretum, Washington Park, the Pittock Mansion, the Audubon Society Sanctuary and Balch Creek. Trails and maintenance roads are accessible year-round to hikers and joggers. Some trails are open to mountain bikers and equestrians.

TriMet MAX and buses serve many trailheads. Visit Forest Park Conservancy at www.forestparkconservancy.org for transit access details, park maps and more.

40-Mile Loop Trail
Portland, Fairview, Gresham, Clackamas, Troutdale

In their 1903 parks plan for Portland, the Olmsted Brothers envisioned an interconnected 40-mile chain of parks, boulevards and greenways. Now, 100 years later the loop totals more than 140 miles and is nearly complete, connecting more than 30 parks in two counties and six cities. The system of earthen trails, bikeways and multiuse paths connects visitors to some of the region's most popular destinations, including the Columbia River, OHSU, the Oregon Zoo and OMSI.

TriMet serves multiple trailheads. Visit www.40mileloop.org for maps and information.

Barton Park
Boring

Located 10 miles east of Clackamas on the Clackamas River, Barton Park offers a variety of recreational opportunities. Overnight visitors will find spacious campgrounds, while day users will enjoy the covered picnic areas. Activities include horseshoes, volleyball and softball, but the park's greatest attraction is the river, which draws anglers and rafters from around the region. The boat ramp is a popular exit point for rafters starting 6 miles upriver at Milo McIver State Park and a popular entry point for those floating downriver 5 miles to Carver.

TriMet bus 31 serves the park entrance at SE Bakers Ferry Road and Highway 224. Visit www.co.clackamas.or.us for maps and information.

Springwater Corridor Trail
Portland, Milwaukie, Gresham, Boring

Acquired in 1990 by the City of Portland, the Springwater Corridor follows a 21 mile railroad grade from Southeast Portland to Boring. The trail offers recreational amenities for walkers, joggers, hikers, cyclists and equestrians. In Portland, the trail follows the Willamette River, passing through Oaks Bottom Wildlife Refuge, before continuing east to Tideman-Johnson Nature Park, Powell Butte Nature Park, Main City Park in Gresham and beyond.

TriMet serves multiple trailheads. See www.portlandonline.com/parks for more information.

Salish Ponds Wetland Park
Fairview

Located between Halsey and Glisan streets at the site of an old rock quarry, the 70 acre Salish Ponds Wetland Park opened in October 1999 and is Fairview's largest city park. Visitors can see hawks, geese, ducks, rabbits, coyotes and other wildlife. The Salish Ponds Trail connects to the Reynolds Middle School campus and the Gresham-Fairview Regional Trail to the west.

Take TriMet bus 77 to 207th Avenue and walk south two blocks to the Salish Ponds Trailhead. Visit www.ci.fairview.or.us for more information.

Clackamette Park
Oregon City

Clackamette Park's beautiful beaches draw visitors from all over the region to lie in the sun or watch wildlife. Nature lovers find sanctuary along wooded paths, while fisherman and swimmers enjoy the converging waters of the Willamette and Clackamas rivers. The Oregon City Skatepark, located near the entrance of the park, features state of the art design.

TriMet buses 32, 33, 34, 79 and 99 traveling along SE McLoughlin Blvd. serve Clackamette Park. Get off at Dunes Drive and walk one block west and one block north to the park entrance at 1955 Clackamette Drive in Oregon City. Visit www.oregoncityparks.org/parks for more information.

Ibach Park
Tualatin

Tualatin's Hedges Creek Greenway and Indian Meadows Greenway converge at Ibach Park. In addition to scenic creekside paths and bridges, Ibach Park features over 19 acres of active recreational opportunities including an award-winning, interactive educational play area. Interpretive amenities include signage and distinctively designed areas reflecting Tualatin's history and pre-history.

Take TriMet bus 96 to SW Ibach Street in Tualatin and walk west 0.5 mile to the park entrance at 10455 SW Ibach Street. Visit www.ci.tualatin.or.us for maps and more information.

Tualatin Hills Nature Park
Beaverton

The Tualatin Hills Nature Park is a 222 acre wildlife preserve in the heart of Beaverton. Consisting of evergreen and deciduous forests, creeks, wetlands, ponds and meadows, the park is home to a variety of wildlife. Of its 5 miles of trails, about 1.5 miles are paved, while the rest are well-maintained soft surface trails. Dogs and other pets are not allowed. The park has an interpretive center with a library, nature store and exhibits. The center offers recreation and nature classes for adults, children and school groups.

The MAX Blue Line's Merlo Road/158th Station brings visitors to the Oak Trailhead. Follow the asphalt trail through the park for 0.75 mile to the visitor center at 15655 SW Millikan Way in Beaverton. Visit www.thprd.org/parks/trails for maps and information.

Tualatin River National Wildlife Refuge
Sherwood

Managed by the U.S. Fish and Wildlife Service, the refuge is located in the Tualatin River floodplain. The area includes a variety of habitats and is home to nearly 200 species of birds and a wide variety of mammals, reptiles, insects, fish and plants. The refuge features a 1-mile year-round nature trail with ADA access, as well as 3 miles of seasonal walking paths, open May 1 through September 30.

TriMet buses 12 and 94 serves the refuge at 19255 SW Pacific Highway in Sherwood. Bicycle parking is provided at the main entrance; however, bicycles are not permitted on refuge trails. Visit www.fws.gov/tualatinriver/ for maps and more information.

Westside Trail/Powerline Trail
Beaverton

The Westside Trail, formerly known as the Beaverton Powerline Trail, will be a continuous multiuse trail from the Tualatin River north to Forest Park and the Willamette River. The completed trail will be 24 miles long and connect to major trails and natural areas. Trail amenities include an ADA-compliant paved surface, natural settings and benches. Currently 5 miles are complete in various segments, including 1.25 miles north of Scholls Ferry Road; between Walker and Jenkins roads; and from Schuepbach Park to Tualatin Hills Nature Park. See www.thprd.com/pdfs/parks/powerlinebrochure.pdf for completed segments.

Visit www.trimet.org or call 503-238-RIDE (7433) to find bus routes serving the various trailheads.

Willamette Park
Portland

On the Willamette River in Southwest Portland, Willamette Park is within easy walking distance of Portland neighborhoods including John's Landing, Fulton, Sellwood, Dunthorpe, Lair Hill and South Waterfront. The park features a paved path along the river and provides an off-street connection between houses and shops on SW Macadam Avenue. In addition to spectacular river views, Willamette Park features a boat ramp, an off-leash dog area and sports fields.

TriMet bus 35 serves Willamette Park. Ride south on SW Macadam Avenue to the stop on SW Nebraska Street. Walk east one block on Nebraska. Go south on SW Beaver Avenue one block to the park entrance. Visit www.portlandonline.com/parks for more information.

●   ●   ●

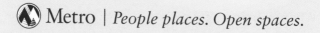
Metro | *People places. Open spaces.*

Metro's Guide to Exploring the Region

- View and print the route maps and descriptions found in this book, with the option to print them at a larger size.

- Learn about walking events and activities.

- Link to local walking maps.

- Discover Portland area walking guidebooks.

- Map your own path and share favorite routes with friends and family.

- Get active with walking clubs and organizations in your community.

Visit Metro's website for information and resources that will keep you walking!

www.oregonmetro.gov/walk

Walking Safety

When exercising, follow a few common-sense tips

Accommodate injuries or limitations.
Listen to your body and slow down if it says so. If you feel pain beyond a mild discomfort, stop the activity and treat the pain. Check with your health care provider for any cautions.

Drink water.
Drink water before, during and after physical activity to prevent dehydration.

General safety guidelines for walking.

- Cross at the corner and use the crosswalk
- Walk against traffic on roads with no sidewalks
- Wear light- or brightly-colored clothing and reflective patches
- Use lights when walking at night
- Watch for turning vehicles
- Look left, right and left again before crossing
- Establish eye contact with drivers and cyclists
- Stay to the right on off-street paths shared with cyclists
- Check the path: watch for uneven pavement, slick surfaces, curbs and ramps
- Be sure your shoes are appropriate for the activity

Kaiser Permanente Wellness Resources

"Healthy Eating, Active Living" are two of the most important ways to improve or maintain your health. That's why it is the theme for Kaiser Permanente's Community Health Initiative. Walking is a cornerstone of this initiative. Walking is simple, requiring no instruction or special equipment, and is an effective way to support a healthy lifestyle. Partnering to create this walking guide is just one way Kaiser Permanente works to help individuals and communities thrive.

Kaiser Permanente is excited to promote walking and alternative modes of transportation and to highlight the health impacts that come from using trails, greenways and natural areas. Through the power of partnership, more people will be walking for health and transportation purposes in Clark, Clackamas, Multnomah and Washington counties.

Before or after you take a walk, take a moment to check out these wellness resources and information.

www.KaiserPermanente.org

Support is only a few mouse clicks away at the Kaiser Permanente Web site, where you can check out class schedules, featured topics, health and drug encyclopedias, and more.

You can also:

- Find an audio library of programs that include "Walking for Health" and "Exercise Smart." Listen online or download them for later use, at www.kp.org/listen
- Figure out your BMI or the number of calories you burn in various activities, at www.kp.org/calculators
- Browse an herb and supplement database, at www.kp.org/naturalmedicines

10,000 Steps® Program

Reap the benefits of a healthier lifestyle with an online program designed to help you increase your physical activity level and work toward a goal of walking 10,000 steps each day. When you sign up, you will receive an interactive, online system to set personal goals, track daily steps and monitor your progress, find quick and healthy meal ideas, and receive daily email tips that provide support. Visit www.10k-steps.com for more information.

Health Resource Centers

Do you need health information? The Kaiser Permanente Health Resource Centers can help.

At a center, you can investigate reference books, watch videos and DVDs, explore Internet resources, select health-education handouts, and buy books and products.

The Health Resource Centers are open to the community Monday through Friday, 9 a.m. to 5:30 p.m., at:

Salmon Creek Medical Office
14406 NE 20th Ave.
Vancouver, WA 98686

Sunset Medical Office
19400 NW Evergreen Parkway
Hillsboro, OR 97124

Acknowledgments

Many organizations, agencies and individuals collaborated to develop this regional guidebook. Cities, counties, park districts and nonprofits contributed walking routes and descriptions. Additional support was provided by Kaiser Permanente, HEAL (Healthy Eating Active Living Partnership), Willamette Pedestrian Coalition, Columbia River Volkssport Club, SW Trails Group, Wilsonville SMART, and the cities of Gresham, Portland and Vancouver. A very special thanks to Rich Cassidy with the city of Portland, and to the many volunteers who checked routes and maps.

Project Team

Laura O. Foster, editor

Eli Castillo and Brad Smith, *Hot Pepper Studios*, design

Eben Dickinson, illustrations

Erik Goetze and Matthew Hampton, *Metro*, maps

Pam Peck, *Metro*, project manager

Elizabeth Adams, Mary Ann Aschenbrenner, Pamela Blackhorse, Dan Kaempff, Sabrina Gogol, Mel Huie, Janice Larson, Hector Osuna, Robert Spurlock, Lia Waiwaiole and Caleb Winter, *Metro*, project support.

About the Editor

Laura O. Foster is the author of *Portland Hill Walks: Twenty Explorations in Parks and Neighborhoods* (2005) and *Portland City Walks: Twenty Explorations In and Around Town* (Fall 2008). She leads walking tours in historic neighborhoods for the City of Portland, the Forest Park Conservancy and other civic groups.

Photo Credits

Pamela Blackhorse, *Land-C Studio* (pp. 68, 220), Eli Castillo, *Hot Pepper Studios* (pp. 28, 32, 36, 44, 48, 110, 118, 122, 126, 138, 150), Jim Cruce (pp. 78, 130), Michael Durham (p. 188), Bruce Forster (p. 226), Mike Houck (p. 191), Cheryl Juetten (p. 60), *Lloyd Center Mall* (p. 52), and *Pacific University* (pp. 200, 201, 204).

Index